The
Four-Sided Cookie

Also by Lorraine Bodger

The
Four-Sided Cookie

55 Recipes for
Delicious Squares and Bars

Written and Illustrated by

Lorraine Bodger

St. Martin's Griffin ✻ New York

ISBN 0-312-20675-5

Design by Maureen Troy

First Edition: January 2000

10   9   8   7   6   5   4   3   2   1

Contents

The
Four-Sided Cookie

Making Squares and Bars

Homemade bars and squares are everything you ever wanted in a cookie. They're bigger and a bit more substantial than most ordinary drop or rolled cookies, and they offer the delicious flavors you love combined with a baking technique that couldn't be easier. Just mix, bake in a *single* pan, cut neatly, and your batch of irresistible cookies is ready to eat.

There are two varieties of bars and squares: The first is a simple batter spread in a pan, then baked and sometimes glazed or frosted. The second kind is a layered cookie, usually with a bottom crust, a filling, and a topping. Whether you're an expert at cookie baking or a first-timer, you'll find either kind a snap to make and a delight to eat.

The following suggestions and guidelines will take you through the process with ease.

- Read the entire recipe before you begin baking.
- Don't skimp on ingredients; use the best quality you can afford.
- Use unsalted (sweet) butter, all-purpose flour, white granulated sugar (unless light or dark brown sugar is specified), large eggs, and ground spices. If the recipe calls for nuts, taste them before adding; nuts must be absolutely fresh, not stale or moldy. Dried fruit, raisins, and currants should be soft. Always use pure vanilla extract—no imitations. Never use chocolate-flavored products; if possible, buy high-quality chocolate such as Callebaut, Lindt, Tobler, Valrhona, or Ghirardelli. When cocoa powder is listed in the ingredients, use pure, unsweetened cocoa powder, not cocoa mix.
- In these recipes, there's no need to sift flour before measuring it.
- Measure ingredients carefully. For liquids, use clear glass or plastic measuring cups; for dry ingredients, use metal cups or measuring spoons that can be leveled off with a knife or spatula.

- To measure dry ingredients (flour, baking powder or soda, granulated sugar, confectioners' sugar, cocoa, spices), spoon into a measuring cup or measuring spoon and level off. To measure light or dark brown sugar, pack it so firmly into a metal measuring cup that it holds its shape when turned out.

- Each recipe in this book requires one of three baking pans: 9 × 9-inch baking pan; 9 × 13-inch baking pan; 10½ × 15½-inch jelly roll pan. Use shiny—not dark—pans, and be sure to use the correct size for each recipe.

- Pans should be baked in the center of the oven, so shift one oven rack to the center slot.

- Preheat the oven for 10 to 15 minutes. Be sure your oven temperature is correct; if it isn't, the baking times given in the recipes won't be reliable. To test your oven temperature, put a mercury-type oven thermometer in the middle of an oven rack placed in the center slot of the oven. Preheat for 15 minutes and then check the thermometer. If the temperature setting disagrees with the reading on the thermometer, adjust the setting up or down accordingly.

- To grease and flour a baking pan, first apply a thin coat of soft butter or margarine to the bottom and sides of the pan; a pastry brush works well for this job. Then sprinkle the greased pan with flour and (working over the sink) tap it briskly while you tilt it back and forth. Tip excess flour into the sink.

- Use an electric mixer for creaming butter and sugar; beat until the sugar is barely grainy. This can take a few minutes, so be patient.

- A food processor is wonderful for chopping nuts and making cookie crumbs, but it is especially useful in preparing the dough for the bottom layers of many bar cookies, as specified in the recipes.

- Spreading the batter or dough evenly in the prepared pan is the most important step in making bar cookies. *Thin batter*: Use a rubber spatula to spread it, then tilt the pan back and forth until evenly distributed. *Thick batter*: Use a rubber spatula to spread it roughly, then use a small metal offset spatula to even it out. *Dough*: Distribute clumps of dough over the bottom of the pan, then pat out to cover the bottom evenly; if the dough is very sticky, either moisten your fingertips or dust them with flour.

- Set your kitchen timer when you put a pan of bar cookies into the oven.

The baking times in the recipes have been carefully tested, so if one baking time is given (for example, 11 minutes), set your timer for that number. If a choice of times is given in the recipe (for example, 8 to 10 minutes), set the timer for the lower number and check the pan when the timer goes off. If the bars are done, as described in the recipe, remove the pan from the oven; if not, continue baking for some or all of the additional number of minutes.

• When the pan of cookies is done, let it cool on a wire rack as instructed in the recipe. Run a sharp (not serrated) knife around the edges of the pan to loosen the dough. Use the same sharp knife to cut the dough into bars or squares according to the recipe recommendation.

• Remove cookies slowly and carefully, starting at any corner and working along the row. The first couple of cookies you remove may crumble a bit; this is normal. A small offset spatula is the best tool for lifting bar cookies out of their pan.

• Cooled bars and squares may be stored in any number of ways: in the pan, tightly covered; individually wrapped in plastic; wrapped in packets of four, eight, or any other desired amount; layered in an airtight container (with layers separated by plastic wrap); in zip-lock bags, either loose or wrapped in plastic; wrapped in plastic, placed in a zip-lock bag, and frozen.

STOCKING THE PANTRY

Keep basic ingredients on hand in your pantry and refrigerator so you'll be able to whip up a panful of bars or squares whenever the fancy takes you. You may also want to stock up on a few of the less basic ingredients, to expand the possibilities for cookie-baking fun.

Basic Ingredients
• Flour (all-purpose)
• Baking powder; baking soda
• Salt

- Sugar (white granulated)
- Light brown sugar
- Unsalted (sweet) butter
- Eggs (large)
- Pure vanilla extract

Other ingredients
- Other sugars: superfine, dark brown, confectioners' (also called powdered sugar)
- Other sweeteners: honey, molasses, light corn syrup
- Nuts: walnuts, pecans, almonds, hazelnuts, pine nuts, macadamias, peanuts
- Almond extract
- Pure almond paste
- Chocolate (in blocks or chunks): unsweetened, semisweet
- Semisweet chocolate chips (regular, miniature)
- Cocoa powder
- Dark and light raisins; currants; other dried fruit
- Sweetened shredded coconut
- Ground spices: cinnamon, ginger, nutmeg, allspice, cloves
- Graham crackers
- Peanut butter

Baking is more fun and a lot easier if you do it with at least some of the right equipment. If you have the following items, you'll be running on all four cylinders.

- ❏ Graduated measuring cups for dry ingredients
- ❏ Glass measuring cup for liquid ingredients
- ❏ Metal measuring spoons
- ❏ Small and large mixing bowls
- ❏ Heavy saucepan for melting chocolate
- ❏ Wooden spoons for mixing by hand
- ❏ Wire whisk
- ❏ Electric mixer with variable speeds (hand-held is fine)
- ❏ Food processor
- ❏ Rubber spatulas for scraping down the sides of the bowls
- ❏ Small and large offset spatulas
- ❏ Oven thermometer (mercury type) for checking and adjusting oven temperature
- ❏ Timer
- ❏ Baking pans (shiny, not dark): 9 × 9-inch square, 9 × 13-inch rectangle, 10½ × 15½-inch jelly roll pan
- ❏ Wire racks, raised on wire feet, for cooling the cookies

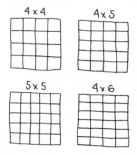

4 x 4   4 x 5

5 x 5   4 x 6

9 × 9-inch pan

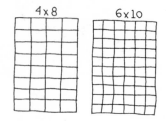

4 x 8   6 x 10

10½ × 15½ -inch pan

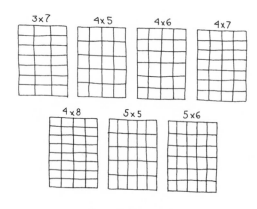

3 x 7   4 x 5   4 x 6   4 x 7

4 x 8   5 x 5   5 x 6

9 × 13-inch pan

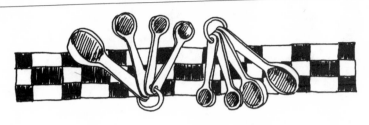

Pinch = a little less than ⅛ teaspoon
⅛ teaspoon = 2 pinches
1 tablespoon = 3 teaspoons
¼ cup = 4 tablespoons
⅓ cup = 5⅓ tablespoons
½ cup = 8 tablespoons
⅔ cup = 10⅔ tablespoons
¾ cup = 12 tablespoons
1 cup = 16 tablespoons
¼ cup butter = ½ stick = 4 tablespoons
½ cup butter = ¼ pound = 1 stick = 8 tablespoons
1 cup butter = ½ pound = 2 sticks = 16 tablespoons

Favorite Squares and Bars

Here's where you'll find your all-time favorite bars and squares: *Chocolate Chip Squares, Classic Blondies, Lemon Squares, Pecan Pie Squares, Cream Cheese Squares,* and *Crunchy Peanut Butter Bars.* You'll also find a few surprises, such as *Almond Toffee Bars, Rocky Road Squares,* and two kinds of melt-in-your-mouth shortbread.

Tip: These are easy recipes—a good place to start if you're new to cookie baking.

Chocolate Chip Squares

If you love traditional chocolate chip cookies, you'll love these chewy squares packed with chips and nuts—and they're a lot easier to make than chocolate chip drop cookies. These are large squares; cut them smaller if you prefer.

1 cup flour
½ teaspoon baking powder
¼ teaspoon salt
½ cup (1 stick) unsalted butter, at room temperature
¼ cup sugar

½ cup packed light brown sugar
1 egg
1 teaspoon vanilla extract
¾ cup semisweet chocolate chips
½ cup chopped walnuts or pecans

1. Preheat the oven to 350°F; grease and flour a 9 × 9-inch baking pan. In a small bowl, stir or whisk together the flour, baking powder, and salt.

2. In a large bowl, cream the butter, sugar, and brown sugar. Add the egg and vanilla and beat well. Gradually add the flour mixture, blending well after each addition. Stir in the chocolate chips and chopped nuts.

3. Spread the batter evenly in the prepared pan.

4. Bake for 25 to 30 minutes, until the top is golden, the edges are brown and pulling away from the sides of the pan, and a toothpick inserted in the center of the pan comes out clean. Let the pan cool completely on a wire rack. Run a sharp knife around the edge of the pan, then cut into 16 squares (4 squares by 4 squares).

Rocky Road Squares

"Rocky road" in the recipe title tells you that this deliciously messy cookie features nuts, marshmallows, and chunks of chocolate (in this case, semisweet chocolate chips) in the batter and on top.

1 cup flour
½ teaspoon baking powder
¼ teaspoon salt
6 tablespoons unsalted butter, at
  room temperature
¾ cup sugar

2 eggs
1 teaspoon vanilla extract
1 cup semisweet chocolate chips
½ cup chopped walnuts or pecans
½ cup miniature marshmallows

1. Preheat the oven to 350°F; grease and flour a 9 × 9-inch baking pan. In a small bowl, stir or whisk together the flour, baking powder, and salt.

2. In a large bowl, cream the butter and sugar. Add the eggs and vanilla and beat well. Gradually add the flour mixture, blending well after each addition. Stir in half of the chocolate chips, half of the chopped nuts, and half of the marshmallows.

3. Spread the batter evenly in the prepared pan.

4. Bake for 20 minutes. Remove the pan from the oven and sprinkle the top evenly with the remaining chocolate chips, nuts, and marshmallows; press lightly with a pancake turner so they stick to the hot dough. Return the pan to the oven and bake for 8 to 10 minutes longer, until the marshmallows are golden. Let the pan cool completely on a wire rack. Run a sharp knife around the edge of the pan, then cut into 25 squares (5 squares by 5 squares), wiping the knife blade between cuts.

Lemon Squares

Here's a cookie dough you can make entirely in your food processor. The cookie crust is rich and sweet, and the lemon topping is tangy and bright.

For the bottom layer:
    1 cup flour stirred with ⅛ teaspoon salt
    ½ cup sugar
    ½ cup (1 stick) cold unsalted butter, cut into pats

For the topping:
    2 eggs
    1 egg yolk
    ⅔ cup sugar
    1½ tablespoons flour
    1 teaspoon grated lemon rind
    ⅓ cup fresh lemon juice
    Confectioners' sugar (optional)

1. Preheat the oven to 375°F; grease and flour a 9 × 9-inch baking pan.
2. Make the bottom layer: Put the flour and sugar in the bowl of a food processor and process to combine. Add the butter and process until the mixture clumps, scraping down the bowl several times. Pat the dough evenly over the bottom of the prepared pan. Bake for 14 to 16 minutes, until the top is dry-looking and lightly browned at the edges. Place the pan on a wire rack to cool. Reduce the oven temperature to 350°F.

3. Make the topping: Put the eggs, egg yolk, sugar, flour, lemon rind, and lemon juice in the food processor bowl (there is no need to wash the bowl after making the bottom layer) and process until well blended. Pour the topping over the cooled dough in the pan.

4. Bake for 16 to 18 minutes longer, until the top is dry and covered with tiny craters (broken bubbles), and the edges are lightly browned; do not overcook. Let the pan cool completely on a wire rack. If you like, sprinkle with 1 or 2 tablespoons of confectioners' sugar sifted through a fine strainer. Run a sharp knife around the edge of the pan, then cut into 25 squares (5 squares by 5 squares), wiping the knife blade between cuts.

Pecan Pie Squares

MAKES 25 SQUARES

These luscious goodies have the classic pecan pie flavor, but you don't have to make a pie to get it. The squares are very rich, so it's a good idea to cut them small.

For the bottom layer:
1 cup flour stirred with ¼ teaspoon salt
½ cup packed light brown sugar
½ cup (1 stick) cold unsalted butter, cut into pats

For the topping:
2 eggs
½ cup light corn syrup
½ cup packed light brown sugar
2 tablespoons unsalted butter, melted and cooled
1 teaspoon vanilla extract
¼ teaspoon salt
¾ cup coarsely chopped toasted pecans

1. Preheat the oven to 350°F; have ready an ungreased 9 × 9-inch baking pan.
2. Make the bottom layer: Put the flour and brown sugar in the bowl of a food processor and pulse several times to combine. Add the butter and process until the mixture clumps, scraping down the bowl several times. With flour-dusted fingers, pat the dough evenly over the bottom of the pan. Bake for 12 to 15 minutes, until lightly browned. Let the pan cool on a wire rack.

3. Make the topping: Put the eggs, corn syrup, brown sugar, melted butter, vanilla, and salt in the food processor bowl (there is no need to wash the bowl after making the bottom layer) and process until well blended. Add the pecans and pulse several times to combine and to chop the pecans into pea-size pieces. Do not overprocess or the pecan pieces will be too small.

4. Pour the topping evenly over the cooled dough in the pan.

5. Bake for 28 to 32 minutes longer, until the topping is set. Let the pan cool completely on a wire rack. Run a sharp knife around the edge of the pan, then cut into 25 squares (5 squares by 5 squares).

10 Hints for Great Bar Cookies

1. Read the ingredients list and take out everything you'll need, including equipment, before you begin.
2. Use the right size pan for optimum results.
3. To bring cold butter to room temperature when you're in a hurry, cut it into thin pats and arrange in one layer on a plate; butter will soften quickly.
4. Do the prep work—melting butter or chocolate, chopping nuts—before you start mixing.
5. Use a soft pastry brush for greasing the pan with either butter or margarine.
6. Don't forget to preheat the oven for at least 10 minutes. Use a kitchen timer to tell you when the oven is ready.
7. When you're beating ingredients with an electric mixer, be sure to scrape down the bowl several times so the ingredients are thoroughly combined. Do the same when you're mixing ingredients in a food processor.

8. Use a rubber spatula to scrape batter into the pan; use a small off-set spatula to spread the batter evenly.

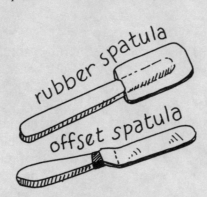

rubber spatula

offset spatula

9. When patting dough into a pan, usually dry fingertips do the job best. If the dough is very buttery, moistening your fingertips or dipping them in flour will keep the dough from sticking to them.
10. Don't forget to set your kitchen timer as soon as you put the pan in the preheated oven.

Almond Toffee Bars

Thin and crisp, with crunchy bits of almond in the soft center—these bars have a sensational flavor, and they're topped with gooey milk chocolate and more crunchy almonds.

1 cup (2 sticks) unsalted butter, at room temperature
½ cup sugar
½ cup packed light brown sugar
1 egg yolk
1 teaspoon vanilla extract
2 cups flour stirred with ¼ teaspoon salt

½ cup chopped almonds (with or without skins), toasted
4 ounces high-quality milk chocolate (bulk or bar, such as Callebaut, Lindt, Valrhona, or Ghirardelli), chopped into chip-size pieces

1. Preheat the oven to 350°F; have ready an ungreased 9 × 13-inch baking pan.

2. In a large bowl, cream the butter, sugar, and brown sugar. Add the egg yolk and vanilla and beat well. Gradually add the flour, blending well after each addition. Stir in half of the chopped almonds.

3. Use a small metal offset spatula to spread the dough evenly in the pan.

4. Bake for 24 to 26 minutes, until the top is lightly browned and puffy; the top will flatten out as it cools. Place the pan on a wire rack, and immediately scatter the milk chocolate pieces evenly over the hot dough. When the chocolate is very soft, in about 2 minutes, spread evenly. Immediately sprinkle with the remaining chopped almonds; press the almonds lightly into the chocolate. Allow to cool completely. Run a sharp knife around the edge of the pan, then cut into 32 bars (4 bars by 8 bars).

Butterscotch Bars

All you need are a few simple ingredients to mix up a rich, super-chewy, unmistakably butterscotch-flavored bar cookie—and it's prepared in a single saucepan. Toasting the walnuts is important for a crunchy texture, so don't skip that bit of preparation.

1 cup flour
1 teaspoon baking powder
¼ teaspoon salt
6 tablespoons unsalted butter
1¼ cups packed light brown sugar
1 egg
1 teaspoon vanilla extract
¾ cup chopped toasted walnuts

1. Preheat the oven to 350°F; grease a 9 × 9-inch baking pan. In a small bowl, stir or whisk together the flour, baking powder, and salt.
2. In a large saucepan over low heat, melt the butter. Turn off the heat and stir in the brown sugar, egg, and vanilla. Gradually add the flour mixture, blending well after each addition. Stir in the toasted walnuts.
3. Spread the batter evenly in the prepared pan.
4. Bake for 21 to 23 minutes, until the top is dry and crisp and a toothpick inserted in the center of the pan comes out clean. Let the pan cool completely on a wire rack. Run a sharp knife around the edge of the pan, then cut into 20 bars (4 bars by 5 bars).

Classic Blondies

The best blondie I've ever tasted—crisp on top, moist in the center, with a wonderful light brown sugar taste and toasty flavor of nuts. If you like, add ½ cup miniature or regular semisweet chocolate chips.

1 cup flour
1 teaspoon baking powder
¼ teaspoon salt
½ cup (1 stick) unsalted butter, at room temperature
½ cup sugar
⅔ cup packed light brown sugar
2 eggs
1 teaspoon vanilla extract
1 cup chopped walnuts or pecans

1. Preheat the oven to 350°F; grease a 9 × 9-inch baking pan. In a small bowl, stir or whisk together the flour, baking powder, and salt.

2. In a large bowl, cream the butter, sugar, and brown sugar. Add the eggs and vanilla and beat well. Gradually add the flour mixture, blending well after each addition. Stir in the chopped nuts.

3. Spread the batter evenly in the prepared pan.

4. Bake for 30 to 35 minutes, until a toothpick inserted in the center of the pan comes out almost clean. Let the pan cool completely on a wire rack. Run a sharp knife around the edge of the pan, then cut into 16 squares (4 squares by 4 squares).

My Grandmother's Easy Marble Squares

Making marbleized squares is easy when you do it my grandmother's way—by melting chocolate chips right on the vanilla batter, and swirling them in with a knife.

1 cup flour
½ teaspoon baking powder
½ teaspoon salt
½ cup (1 stick) unsalted butter, at room temperature
6 tablespoons sugar

6 tablespoons packed light brown sugar
1 egg
½ teaspoon vanilla extract
½ cup chopped walnuts
1 cup semisweet chocolate chips

1. Preheat the oven to 375°F; grease a 9 × 9-inch baking pan. In a small bowl, stir or whisk together the flour, baking powder, and salt.

2. In a large bowl, cream the butter, sugar, and brown sugar. Add the egg and vanilla and beat well. Gradually add the flour mixture, blending well after each addition. Stir in the walnuts.

3. Spread the batter evenly in the prepared pan. Scatter the chocolate chips evenly over the batter.

4. Place the pan in the oven for *4 to 5 minutes,* until the chips soften. Zigzag a knife through the soft chips and batter, bringing some of the batter up and over the chocolate, to marbleize; don't overmix or you'll lose the marbled look.

5. Return the pan to the oven and bake for 20 to 22 minutes, until the top is golden, the edges are browned, and a toothpick inserted in the center of the pan comes out clean. Let the pan cool completely on a wire rack. Run a sharp knife around the edge of the pan, then cut into 25 squares (5 squares by 5 squares).

Glazed Vanilla Bars

MAKES 28 BARS

When you want a customized taste and look, this is the super-simple bar cookie to make. These vanilla-flavored bars can be topped with chocolate, rum, lemon, or any other glaze you like (see pages 121 to 126) and decorated to suit your fancy—with sprinkles, chopped nuts, sweetened coconut, and so on. See Simple Decorations for Bar Cookies, page 76, for lots more ideas.

1 cup (2 sticks) unsalted butter, at room temperature
1 cup sugar
1 egg
1 tablespoon vanilla extract
2 cups flour stirred with ½ teaspoon salt
¾ to 1 cup glaze (your choice, pages 122 to 126)
Decorations (your choice or optional): miniature chocolate chips; grated
    chocolate; multicolored or chocolate sprinkles; multicolored dots; colored
    sugar; chopped nuts; toasted coconut

1. Preheat the oven to 350°F; grease and flour a 9 × 13-inch baking pan.
2. In a large bowl, cream the butter and sugar. Add the egg and vanilla and beat well. Gradually add the flour, blending well after each addition.
3. Spread the batter evenly in the prepared pan.
4. Bake for 23 to 26 minutes, until the top is lightly browned and a toothpick inserted in the center comes out clean. Place the pan on a wire rack to cool completely.
5. Using a small spatula, spread glaze evenly over the baked dough. If you want to decorate, immediately sprinkle decorations onto the still-tacky glaze;

larger decorations such as chocolate chips or chopped nuts should be pressed lightly into the glaze. Let the glaze set at room temperature or in the refrigerator. Carefully run a sharp knife around the edge of the pan, then cut into 28 bars (4 bars by 7 bars), wiping the knife blade between cuts.

Bar Cookie Mix-and-Match

Some of the ingredients in a bar cookie recipe can't be altered, but others lend themselves perfectly to substitutions. Ingredients that are added to batter for texture (such as semisweet chocolate chips, chopped nuts, or raisins), and toppings that are added after baking (such as glazes or decorations) can easily be altered to suit your personal preference. After all, tastes vary, and you may like white chocolate chips more than semisweet chocolate chips, pecans better than walnuts, light raisins more than dark, vanilla glaze instead of chocolate. Feel free to make a change.

Toasted Coconut Squares

MAKES 25 SQUARES

You can't miss the terrific coconut flavor in these rich, chewy squares. Great for snacks, or serve them for dessert with a tropical fruit salad of melon, pineapple, and mangoes.

1 cup flour
½ teaspoon baking powder
¼ teaspoon salt
1½ cups sweetened shredded
   coconut

½ cup (1 stick) unsalted butter, at
   room temperature
1 cup packed light brown sugar
1 egg
1½ teaspoons vanilla extract

1. Preheat the oven to 350°F; grease and flour a 9 × 9-inch baking pan. In a small bowl, stir or whisk together the flour, baking powder, and salt.

2. Toast the coconut: Spread the coconut on an ungreased jelly roll pan or baking sheet and bake for 8 to 15 minutes, until lightly browned; stir the coconut around at least twice so it browns evenly, watching carefully to prevent burning; set aside to cool.

3. In a large bowl, cream the butter and brown sugar. Add the egg and vanilla and beat well. Gradually add the flour mixture, blending well after each addition. Stir in the toasted coconut.

4. Spread the batter evenly in the prepared pan.

5. Bake for 23 to 25 minutes, until the top is brown and crisp, and a toothpick inserted in the center of the pan comes out clean. Let the pan cool completely on a wire rack. Run a sharp knife around the edge of the pan, then cut into 25 squares (5 squares by 5 squares).

The Great Graham Cracker–Chocolate Chip Pan Cookie

MAKES 30 BARS

One of the most popular pan cookies ever invented, and it requires only five ingredients. Let your kids make these treats, with a little adult supervision during the baking step.

¾ cup (1 ½ sticks) unsalted butter
2½ cups graham cracker crumbs
1 cup chopped walnuts or pecans
1 cup semisweet chocolate chips
1 14-ounce can sweetened condensed milk

1. Preheat the oven to 350°F; have ready an ungreased 9 × 13-inch baking pan.
2. Make the bottom layer: In a large saucepan, melt the butter. Stir in the graham cracker crumbs. Press two thirds of the mixture into the ungreased pan, in an even layer.
3. Make the topping: Sprinkle first the nuts and then the chocolate chips evenly over the crumbs in the pan. Pour the sweetened condensed milk evenly over the nuts and chips. Scatter the remaining graham cracker mixture evenly over the condensed milk.
4. Bake for 23 to 25 minutes, until the top is golden brown and the edges are firm. Let the pan cool completely on a wire rack. Run a sharp knife around the edge of the pan, then cut into 30 bars (5 bars by 6 bars).

Brown Sugar Shortbread

Shortbread is a variation on bar cookies—a soft dough patted out by hand on a baking sheet, chilled, cut into bars, and baked. Only four ingredients are needed here for a tender, crisp, not-too-sweet cookie.

1 cup (2 sticks) unsalted butter, at room temperature
½ cup packed light brown sugar
1 teaspoon vanilla extract
2 cups flour stirred with ⅛ teaspoon salt

1. In a large bowl, cream the butter, brown sugar, and vanilla. Gradually add the flour, blending well after each addition, to make a soft dough.
2. With flour-dusted hands, place the dough on an ungreased baking sheet and pat it out to an 8 × 9-inch rectangle. Use the edge of a ruler to score the dough in 1 × 2-inch bars, as shown. Use a fork to prick each bar 3 or 4 times. Cover tightly with plastic wrap and refrigerate for 1 hour, or until firm.

3. Preheat the oven to 350°F; have ready an additional ungreased baking sheet. Cut the chilled dough into bars, following the scored lines, and use a spatula to place them 1 inch apart on the baking sheets.

4. If possible, bake only 1 sheet at a time in the center of the oven for 16 to 18 minutes, until lightly colored. If necessary, bake both sheets at the same time, 1 sheet on the middle shelf and 1 on the shelf above, for 10 minutes; then reverse the positions of the 2 baking sheets in the oven and bake for 6 to 8 minutes longer, until lightly colored. Do not overbake; the bars should not brown. Let the bars cool on the baking sheet for 2 or 3 minutes, then carefully transfer to wire racks to finish cooling.

Lemon–Poppy Seed Shortbread

MAKES 36 BARS

Crisp, buttery shortbread with a light essence of lemon and the crunch of poppy seeds.

Tip: Use 6 teaspoons (2 tablespoons) grated rind if you prefer a more intense lemon flavor.

1 cup (2 sticks) unsalted butter, at room temperature
½ cup superfine sugar
1 teaspoon vanilla extract
4 to 6 teaspoons grated lemon rind
2 cups flour stirred with ⅛ teaspoon salt
2 tablespoons poppy seeds

1. In a large bowl, cream the butter, sugar, vanilla, and lemon rind. Gradually add the flour, blending well after each addition, to make a soft dough. Stir in the poppy seeds.

2. With flour-dusted hands, place the dough on an ungreased baking sheet and pat it out to an 8 × 9-inch rectangle. Use the edge of a ruler to score the dough in 1 × 2-inch bars, as shown. Use a fork to prick each bar 3 or 4 times. Cover tightly with plastic wrap and refrigerate for 1 hour, or until firm.

3. Preheat the oven to 350°F; have ready an additional ungreased baking sheet. Cut the chilled dough into bars, following the scored lines, and use a spatula to place them 1 inch apart on the baking sheets.

4. If possible, bake only 1 sheet at a time in the center of the oven for 17 to 19 minutes, until lightly colored. If necessary, bake both sheets at the same time, 1 sheet on the middle shelf and 1 on the shelf above, for 12 minutes; then reverse the positions of the 2 baking sheets in the oven and bake for 5 to 7 minutes longer, until lightly colored. Do not overbake; the bars should not brown. Let the bars cool on the baking sheet for 2 or 3 minutes, then carefully transfer to wire racks to finish cooling.

Cream Cheese Squares

Everyone loves these layered squares—walnut cookie crust slathered with a sweet cream cheese mixture and topped with a sprinkling of crumbs. It's all done in a food processor, as easy as pie.

For the bottom layer:
1 cup flour
¼ cup sugar
¼ teaspoon salt
6 tablespoons cold unsalted butter, cut into pats
½ cup chopped walnuts

For the filling:
8 ounces cream cheese, at room temperature
6 tablespoons sugar
1 tablespoon fresh lemon juice
1 tablespoon milk or water
½ teaspoon vanilla extract
1 egg

1. Preheat the oven to 350°F; grease a 9 × 9-inch baking pan.
2. Make the bottom layer: Put the flour, sugar, and salt in the bowl of a food processor and pulse several times to combine. Add the butter and process until the mixture clumps, scraping down the bowl several times. Add the walnuts and process until the walnuts are small pieces and the mixture is crumbly. Reserve ½ cup of the flour mixture. Pat the remaining flour mixture evenly

over the bottom of the prepared pan. Bake for 14 minutes, until the top is dry and moderately firm to the touch. Place the pan on a wire rack to cool.

3. Make the filling: Put the cream cheese, sugar, lemon juice, milk (or water), vanilla, and egg in the food processor bowl (there's no need to wash the bowl after making the bottom layer) and process until smooth. Pour the filling evenly over the cooled dough in the pan. Sprinkle the reserved flour mixture evenly over the filling.

4. Bake for 26 to 30 minutes longer, until the top is dry. The cream cheese filling will be soft when hot, but it will firm up somewhat as it cools; it should still be creamy when cool. Place the pan on a wire rack to cool completely. Run a sharp knife around the edge of the pan, then cut into 25 squares (5 squares by 5 squares), wiping the knife blade between cuts.

Crunchy Peanut Butter Bars

For anyone who loves peanut butter, here's a crisp, pretty bar with a light but definite peanut flavor and plenty of chopped peanuts on top. Great for snacks.

1 cup flour
½ teaspoon baking powder
¼ teaspoon salt
½ cup (1 stick) unsalted butter, at room temperature
⅓ cup crunchy peanut butter

½ cup sugar
½ cup packed light brown sugar
1 egg
1 teaspoon vanilla extract
½ cup chopped unsalted peanuts

1. Preheat the oven to 350°F; grease a 9 × 13-inch baking pan. In a small bowl, stir or whisk together the flour, baking powder, and salt.

2. In a large bowl, cream the butter, peanut butter, sugar, and brown sugar. Add the egg and vanilla and beat well. Gradually add the flour mixture, blending well after each addition. Stir in half of the chopped peanuts.

3. Spread the batter evenly in the prepared pan. Sprinkle the remaining chopped peanuts over the batter and press them down lightly so they are embedded in the batter.

4. Bake for 19 to 21 minutes, until the top is lightly browned and a toothpick inserted in the center of the pan comes out clean. Let the pan cool completely on a wire rack. Run a sharp knife around the edge of the pan, then cut into 32 bars (4 bars by 8 bars).

Chocolate Squares and Bars

For the chocolate lover in each of us, here are eleven recipes for fabulous chocolate bars and squares of all kinds. They range from the simple *Cocoa-Hazelnut Bars* to the fancy *Black-and-White Bars*, the super-fudgy *Fudge Fingers* to the more cakelike *Cocoa Bars with Caramel-Pecan Glaze*, the dark *Double Chocolate Decadence Squares* to the lighter *Chocolate Squares with Ricotta Topping*. And don't miss *Mint Chocolate Squares* or *Chocolate-Bourbon Bars with Pecan Crust*. There's something for everyone—even a no-bake recipe for hot summer days.

Fudge Fingers

MAKES 24 BARS

These bars are dark, moist, and chock-full of toasted pecans, with a lick of coffee and brown sugar to intensify the chocolate flavor. Totally irresistible—a chocolate-lover's delight.

6 tablespoons flour
6 tablespoons cocoa powder, sifted
¼ teaspoon salt
¾ cup (1½ sticks) unsalted butter
2 tablespoons light corn syrup
¾ cup sugar

¼ cup packed light brown sugar
1 teaspoon vanilla extract
3 eggs
1 tablespoon instant coffee granules dissolved in 1 tablespoon boiling water
1 cup chopped toasted pecans

1. Preheat the oven to 350°F; grease and flour a 9 × 9-inch baking pan. In a small bowl, stir or whisk together the flour, cocoa, and salt.

2. In a large saucepan, melt the butter and corn syrup. Allow to cool until warm. *Whisk* in the sugar, brown sugar, and vanilla. Transfer the butter mixture to a large bowl. Whisk in the eggs 1 at a time, then whisk in the coffee. Add the flour mixture and *stir* just until mixed. Stir in the chopped pecans.

3. Spread the batter evenly in the prepared pan.

4. Bake for 28 to 32 minutes, until a toothpick inserted in the center of the pan comes out clean. Let the pan cool completely on a wire rack. Run a sharp knife around the edge of the pan, then cut into 24 bars (4 bars by 6 bars), wiping the knife blade between cuts.

Almond Brownie Squares

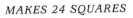

MAKES 24 SQUARES

Thin, crisp, scrumptious brownies. The pan of chocolate dough is studded generously with chunks of almond that become crunchy as they bake. Cut evenly into squares, as suggested, or cut into large pieces and break into any size you like.

¾ cup flour
¼ teaspoon baking powder
¼ teaspoon salt
½ cup (1 stick) unsalted butter
3 ounces unsweetened chocolate, chopped

1 cup sugar
1 teaspoon vanilla extract
2 eggs
1 cup coarsely chopped blanched almonds

1. Preheat the oven to 350°F; grease and flour a 9 × 13-inch baking pan. In a small bowl, stir or whisk together the flour, baking powder, and salt.

2. In a medium-size heavy saucepan over low heat, melt the butter and unsweetened chocolate, whisking until blended and smooth. Transfer to a large bowl, add the sugar and vanilla, and blend well. Whisk in the eggs and then the flour mixture.

3. Spread the batter evenly in the prepared pan. Scatter the almonds evenly over the batter.

4. Bake for 18 to 22 minutes, until the top is firm to the touch and a toothpick inserted in the center of the pan comes out almost clean. Let the pan cool completely on a wire rack. Run a knife around the edge of the pan, then cut into 24 squares (4 squares by 6 squares) or cut into large pieces, between the almonds, and then break into smaller pieces.

Hot Tips: Bar Cookie Desserts

Use your favorite bar cookies as the bases for some fabulous desserts for special occasions such as dinner parties, birthday celebrations, summer patio parties, and holiday feasts.

Cut the cookies slightly larger than usual, to make a generous dessert. Place one cookie on a dessert plate, add a small scoop of sorbet or ice cream or a small serving of fresh fruit, and top with a garnish—chopped nuts, chocolate sauce, fruit sauce, chocolate chips. Here are some possibilities:

- Cream Cheese Squares (page 30) + lemon sorbet + chopped fresh mint
- Toasted Coconut Squares (page 24) + pineapple sorbet + chopped macadamia nuts
- Cocoa-Hazelnut Bars (page 48) + chocolate ice cream + chopped hazelnuts

- Chocolate Chip Squares (page 10) + vanilla ice cream + fudge sauce
- Chocolate Cheesecake Bars (page 38) + coffee ice cream + chopped pecans
- Pear-Almond Squares (page 84) + butter almond ice cream + miniature chocolate chips
- Coconut-Almond Squares (page 114) + sliced fresh mangoes and pineapple + drizzle of almond liqueur
- Glazed Vanilla Bars (page 22) + sliced fresh peaches or nectarines + strawberry sauce
- Lemon Squares (page 12) + fresh berries + custard sauce

Chocolate Cheesecake Bars

MAKES 20 BARS

A traditional graham cracker crust enriched with ground pecans, under a smooth, dense chocolate cream cheese layer. Satisfying and indulgent, but not overly sweet.

For the bottom layer:
⅔ cup graham cracker crumbs
½ cup flour
¼ cup sugar
½ cup ground pecans
½ cup (1 stick) unsalted butter, melted and cooled

For the topping:
8 ounces cream cheese, at room temperature
¼ cup sugar
1 egg
1 egg yolk
1 teaspoon vanilla extract
⅓ cup sour cream
3 ounces high-quality semisweet chocolate (such as Callebaut, Lindt, Valrhona, or Ghirardelli), melted and cooled

1. Preheat the oven to 350°F; grease a 9 × 9-inch baking pan.
2. Make the bottom layer: In a medium-size bowl, stir together the graham cracker crumbs, flour, sugar, and ground pecans. Add the melted butter and stir well. Firmly pat the mixture in an even layer over the bottom of the prepared

pan. Bake for 15 minutes, until the top is dry and the edges are brown. Let the pan cool on a wire rack.

3. Make the topping: In a large bowl, beat the cream cheese and sugar until very smooth. Add the egg, egg yolk, vanilla, sour cream, and melted chocolate and beat well. Spread the topping evenly over the cooled layer in the pan.

4. Bake for 28 to 32 minutes longer, until the top is dry and resilient to the touch; a toothpick inserted in the center of the pan will have soft batter on it. The top may develop a crack or two, just like homemade cheesecake. Let the pan cool completely on a wire rack. Run a sharp knife around the edge of the pan, then cut into 20 bars (4 bars by 5 bars), wiping the knife blade between cuts.

Double Chocolate Decadence Squares

MAKES 25 SQUARES

Chocolate, nothing but chocolate. This bar is thicker than many, almost like a dense chocolate cake with a delicious bittersweet chocolate glaze. It's rich, so it should be cut into not-too-large squares.

½ cup (1 stick) unsalted butter
½ cup light corn syrup
5 ounces high-quality semisweet chocolate (such as Callebaut, Lindt, Valrhona, or Ghirardelli), chopped
¾ cup sugar

1 teaspoon vanilla extract
3 eggs
1 cup flour stirred with
    ¼ teaspoon salt
Bittersweet Chocolate Glaze (page 124)

1. Preheat the oven to 350°F; grease and flour a 9 × 9-inch baking pan.
2. In a medium-size saucepan over low heat, melt the butter, corn syrup, and chocolate, stirring until blended and smooth. Transfer to a large bowl and stir in the sugar and vanilla. Add the eggs 1 at a time, beating well after each addition. Gradually add the flour, blending well after each addition.
3. Spread the batter evenly in the prepared pan.
4. Bake for 30 to 33 minutes, until the top is dry and crisp, and a toothpick inserted in the center of the pan comes out almost clean. Allow the pan to cool completely on a wire rack.
5. Spread as much glaze as you like over the dough, in an even layer, and let the glaze set at room temperature or in the refrigerator. Run a sharp knife around the edge of the pan, then cut into 25 squares (5 squares by 5 squares), wiping the knife blade between cuts.

Cocoa Bars with Caramel-Pecan Glaze

MAKES 32 BARS

You won't need to fool around with tricky melted sugar to make the caramel glaze for this brownie-type bar cookie—simply melt the vanilla caramels and add chopped pecans for crunch.

⅔ cup flour
½ cup cocoa powder, sifted
½ teaspoon baking powder
¼ teaspoon salt
½ cup (1 stick) unsalted butter, at room temperature

1 cup sugar
2 eggs
1 teaspoon vanilla extract
18 vanilla caramels
2 tablespoons milk
½ cup chopped toasted pecans

1. Preheat the oven to 350°F; grease a 9 × 13-inch baking pan. In a small bowl, stir or whisk together the flour, cocoa, baking powder, and salt.

2. In a large bowl, cream the butter and sugar. Add the eggs and vanilla and beat well. Gradually add the flour mixture, blending well after each addition.

3. Spread the batter evenly in the prepared pan.

4. Bake for 24 to 26 minutes, until the top is dry and a toothpick inserted in the center of the pan comes out clean. Let the pan cool for 5 to 10 minutes, until warm; warm dough will make it easy to spread the caramel glaze evenly.

5. In a small saucepan over medium-low heat, stir the caramels and milk until melted and smooth. Stir in the chopped pecans. Spread the glaze evenly over the warm dough in the pan and let it set at room temperature or in the refrigerator. Run a sharp knife around the edge of the pan, then cut into 32 bars (4 bars by 8 bars).

Mint Chocolate Squares

Better than chocolate-covered after-dinner mints: mouth-watering little layered squares of rich chocolate cookie topped with pale green, minty icing and drizzled with chocolate glaze.

For the bottom layer:
½ cup (1 stick) unsalted butter
2 ounces unsweetened chocolate, chopped
1 cup sugar
2 eggs
½ cup flour stirred with ¼ teaspoon salt

For the topping:
3 tablespoons unsalted butter, at room temperature
2 tablespoons milk
1 ½ cups sifted confectioners' sugar
½ teaspoon peppermint extract
Green food coloring

For the glaze:
2 tablespoons unsalted butter
1 tablespoon heavy cream or milk
2 ounces high-quality semisweet chocolate (such as Callebaut, Lindt, Valrhona, or Ghirardelli), chopped

1. Preheat the oven to 350°F; grease and flour a 9 × 9-inch baking pan.

2. Make the bottom layer: In a small saucepan over low heat, melt the butter and chocolate, stirring until blended and smooth; set aside to cool. In a large bowl, beat the sugar and eggs until thick and pale. Add the cooled chocolate mixture and beat well. Gradually add the flour, blending well after each addition. Spread the batter evenly in the prepared pan. Bake for 20 to 24 minutes, until a toothpick inserted in the center of the pan comes out clean. Let the pan cool completely on a wire rack.

3. Make the topping: In a medium-size bowl, beat together the butter, milk, and confectioners' sugar until smooth. Beat in the peppermint extract and enough food coloring to make a pale green; start with just a tiny bit of coloring and add more as needed. Spread the topping evenly over the cooled dough in the pan. Cover with plastic wrap and chill until the topping is firm.

4. Make the glaze: In a small saucepan over low heat, melt the butter, cream, and chocolate, stirring until smooth. Drizzle the glaze over the topping. Cover and chill again until firm. Run a sharp knife around the edge of the pan, then cut into 25 squares (5 squares by 5 squares).

Chocolate Squares
with Ricotta Topping

MAKES 25 SQUARES

One of my favorites: a luscious layer of chocolate topped with mellow, sweet ricotta cheese that's laced with miniature chocolate chips. During baking the chocolate bubbles up into the ricotta topping to make a beautiful dark-and-light surface.

For the bottom layer:
1/2 cup flour
1/3 cup cocoa powder, sifted
1/2 teaspoon baking powder
1/4 teaspoon salt
1/2 cup (1 stick) unsalted butter, at room temperature
1 cup sugar
2 eggs
1 teaspoon vanilla extract

For the topping:
3/4 cup ricotta cheese
2 tablespoons unsalted butter, at room temperature
1/4 cup sugar
1 egg
1 tablespoon flour
1/2 teaspoon vanilla extract
1/3 cup miniature semisweet chocolate chips

1. Preheat the oven to 350°F; grease and flour a 9 × 9-inch baking pan.

2. Make the bottom layer: In a small bowl, stir or whisk together the flour, cocoa, baking powder, and salt. In a large bowl, cream the butter and sugar. Add the eggs and vanilla and beat well. Gradually add the flour mixture, blending well after each addition. Spread the batter evenly in the prepared pan.

3. Make the topping: In a large bowl, combine the ricotta cheese, butter, and sugar and beat well. Add the egg, flour, and vanilla and beat again until smooth and creamy. Stir in the chocolate chips.

4. Drop spoonfuls of the topping on the unbaked batter in the baking pan and use a spatula to spread it carefully in an even layer.

5. Bake for 28 to 32 minutes, until the top looks dry and a toothpick inserted in the center of the pan comes out clean; the top will be a rough pattern of dark chocolate batter and light ricotta topping. Let the pan cool completely on a wire rack. Run a sharp knife around the edge of the pan, then cut into 25 squares (5 squares by 5 squares), wiping the knife blade between cuts.

Black-and-White Bars

MAKES 20 BARS

Three layers make this bar a delicious treat—a dark chocolate base topped with a creamy cream cheese filling, with mocha glaze to finish it off.

For the bottom layer:
1 1/4 cups flour
1/4 cup cocoa powder, sifted
1/8 teaspoon salt
1/2 cup (1 stick) unsalted butter, at room temperature
1/2 cup sugar
1 egg
1/2 teaspoon vanilla extract

For the topping:
6 ounces cream cheese, at room temperature
2 tablespoons unsalted butter, at room temperature
1/2 cup sugar
1 egg
1/2 teaspoon vanilla extract
3 tablespoons flour

Mocha Glaze (page 124)

1. Preheat the oven to 350°; grease a 9 × 9-inch baking pan.
2. Make the bottom layer: In a small bowl, stir or whisk together the flour, cocoa, and salt. In a large bowl, cream the butter and sugar. Add the egg and

vanilla and beat well. Gradually add the flour mixture, blending well after each addition. Spread the batter evenly in the prepared pan. Bake for 14 minutes, then set aside on a wire rack to cool.

3. Make the topping: In a large bowl, beat the cream cheese, butter, and sugar until smooth. Add the egg and vanilla and blend well. Add the flour and blend again. Spread the topping evenly over the baked bottom layer.

4. Bake for 20 to 22 minutes longer, until the top is dry and the edges are golden. Let the pan cool completely on a wire rack. Spread the glaze evenly over the filling and allow to set at room temperature or in the refrigerator. Run a sharp knife around the edge of the pan, then use the same knife, dipped in hot water, to cut into 20 bars (4 bars by 5 bars).

Cocoa-Hazelnut Bars

The distinct flavor of hazelnuts and a kiss of rum make this an elegant cookie—perfect for a dinner party dessert, especially when paired with fruit or sorbet.

½ cup flour
1 cup ground skinned hazelnuts
⅓ cup cocoa powder, sifted
¼ teaspoon salt
2 eggs
¾ cup sugar
2 tablespoons dark or light rum
Confectioners' sugar

1. Preheat the oven to 350°F; grease and flour a 9 × 9-inch baking pan. In a small bowl, stir or whisk together the flour, ground hazelnuts, cocoa, and salt.

2. In a large bowl, beat the eggs until light and lemon-colored. Add the sugar and beat until thick. Add the rum and beat again. Gradually stir in the flour mixture, blending well after each addition.

3. Spread the batter evenly in the prepared pan.

4. Bake for 18 to 22 minutes, until the top is firm to the touch and a toothpick inserted in the center of the pan comes out clean. Allow to cool completely, then dust the top with confectioners' sugar sifted through a fine strainer. Run a sharp knife around the edge of the pan, then cut into 24 bars (4 bars by 6 bars).

No-Bake Chocolate-Marshmallow Bars

MAKES 24 BARS

Chocolate cookies that kids will love—gooey little bars chock-full of marshmallows and topped with plenty of chocolate glaze. These are great to make on a hot day (when you don't want to turn on the oven) and stash in the refrigerator for snacking.

¾ cup (1½ sticks) unsalted butter
½ cup sugar
2 eggs, beaten
1 teaspoon vanilla extract
2½ cups finely crushed chocolate graham cracker crumbs
2 cups miniature marshmallows
1 cup semisweet chocolate chips

1. Grease a 9 × 9-inch baking pan.
2. In a large saucepan, melt the butter. Remove from the heat and stir in the sugar and eggs. Return the saucepan to medium-low heat. Cook, stirring often but gently, until thickened, 8 to 10 minutes. Remove from the heat and stir in the vanilla. Stir in the cookie crumbs and marshmallows.
3. Spread the mixture evenly in the prepared pan.
4. Chill until firm, about 1 hour.
5. In a small saucepan over very low heat, melt the chocolate chips, stirring until smooth. Spread evenly over the chilled layer in the pan. Chill again until firm. Run a sharp knife around the edge of the pan, then cut into 24 bars (4 bars by 6 bars).

Chocolate-Bourbon Bars
with Pecan Crust

MAKES 32 BARS

These sensational bars start with a cookie layer enriched with pecans, which is topped with a dark puddinglike layer of bourbon-spiked chocolate. The light brown top gets crisp during baking, making an appealing contrast of textures.

For the bottom layer:
1 1/4 cups flour
1/2 teaspoon baking powder
1/4 teaspoon salt
1/4 cup sugar
1/2 cup (1 stick) cold unsalted butter, cut into pats
1 cup finely chopped pecans

For the topping:
2 ounces high-quality semisweet chocolate (such as Callebaut, Lindt, Valrhona, or Ghirardelli), chopped
1/4 cup (1/2 stick) unsalted butter
3 eggs
1 cup packed light brown sugar
2 tablespoons bourbon
1 teaspoon vanilla extract

1. Preheat the oven to 350°F; have ready an ungreased 9 × 13-inch baking pan.

2. Make the bottom layer: Put the flour, baking powder, salt, and sugar in the bowl of a food processor and process to combine. Add the butter and process until the mixture begins to clump, scraping down the bowl several times. Add the chopped pecans and pulse several times to blend. With moistened fingers, pat the dough evenly over the bottom of the ungreased baking pan.

3. Make the topping: In a small saucepan over low heat, melt the chocolate and butter, stirring until smooth. Set aside to cool until warm. In a large bowl, combine the eggs, brown sugar, bourbon, and vanilla and beat well. Add the warm chocolate mixture and beat again. Pour the topping over the dough in the pan.

4. Bake for 26 to 30 minutes, until the top is light brown and crisp. Allow to cool completely on a wire rack. Run a sharp knife around the edge of the pan, then cut into 32 bars (4 bars by 8 bars).

Hot Tips: Chocolate

It's always smart to use the best ingredients you can afford—and it's especially smart with chocolate. If you've never tried baking with premium chocolate, you're in for a treat, because great chocolate makes a great bar cookie.

- Use premium chocolate whenever a recipe calls for high-quality semisweet or unsweetened chocolate.
- Scout your local gourmet shop or other fine food store for Callebaut, Lindt, Tobler, Valrhona, or Ghirardelli chocolate; buy them in blocks or bars.
- If you can't locate the premium brands, the less expensive Baker's, Dove, Hershey's, and Nestlé chocolate are widely available in supermarkets and groceries.
- Use packaged semisweet chocolate chips only when chips are required; do not use packaged chips when *melted* chocolate is listed as an ingredient.
- Store all chocolate in a cool, dry place—not the refrigerator.

Snack Squares and Bars

Try the hearty, flavorful recipes in this section when you want great lunchbox treats, after-school snacks, afternoon pick-me-ups, and midnight munchies. *Granola-Date Bars, Currant Squares, Hermit Bars*, and *Chewy Fruit and Nut Squares* feature a variety of dried fruits; *Almond-Cinnamon Bars, Maple-Walnut Squares*, and *Honey-Almond Strips* are chock-full of crunchy nuts. If you like a spicy cookie, you'll love *Carrot Spice Squares with Cream Cheese Frosting*, and *Ginger-Molasses Bars*, too. These bars and squares will give you a real lift just when you need it.

Carrot Spice Squares with Cream Cheese Frosting

If you're a fan of carrot cake, you'll love these squares. They're nice and spicy, loaded with raisins and nuts, and finished off with traditional cream cheese frosting.

1¾ cups flour
1 teaspoon baking soda
½ teaspoon salt
1 teaspoon cinnamon
½ teaspoon ground nutmeg
½ teaspoon ground ginger
½ cup neutral vegetable oil (corn, safflower, canola, or sunflower)
½ cup milk
1 egg
1 cup packed light brown sugar
¾ cup finely shredded carrot
½ cup light or dark raisins
½ cup chopped walnuts

For the frosting:

3 ounces cream cheese, at room temperature
1 tablespoon milk or cream
1 teaspoon vanilla extract
2 cups sifted confectioners' sugar

1. Preheat the oven to 375°F; grease and flour a 9 × 13-inch baking pan. In a medium-size bowl, stir or whisk together the flour, baking soda, salt, and spices.

2. In a large bowl, combine the oil, milk, and egg and beat well. Add the brown sugar and beat again. Gradually add the flour mixture, blending well after each addition. Stir in the shredded carrot, raisins, and walnuts.

3. Spread the batter evenly in the prepared pan.

4. Bake for 18 to 22 minutes, until the top is dry and a toothpick inserted in the center of the pan comes out clean. Let the pan cool completely on a wire rack. Do not cut yet.

5. Make the frosting: In a medium-size bowl, beat the cream cheese, milk (or cream), and vanilla until smooth. Gradually beat in the confectioners' sugar until smooth.

6. Spread the frosting evenly on the cooled layer in the pan. Run a sharp knife around the edge of the pan, then cut into 24 squares (4 squares by 6 squares), wiping the knife blade between cuts. Keep refrigerated until serving.

Granola-Date Bars

A sensational snack bar made from a crunchy granola batter and soft, sweet date filling, with a topping of more crunchy batter. Use the simplest granola you can find—nuts and raisins are fine, but seeds, dried fruits, and other ingredients would be overdoing it for this cookie.

For the filling:
8 ounces pitted dates, chopped or snipped into small pieces
½ cup water
2 tablespoons honey
1 teaspoon vanilla extract

For the bottom layer and topping:
1½ cups flour
1½ cups plain granola
½ teaspoon baking soda
¼ teaspoon salt
¾ cup packed light brown sugar
¾ cup (1½ sticks) cold unsalted butter, cut into pats

1. Preheat the oven to 375°F; have ready an ungreased 9 × 13-inch baking pan.
2. Make the filling: In a saucepan over medium heat, combine the dates, water, and honey. Bring to a boil, then reduce the heat and simmer, stirring constantly, until thick, about 3 minutes. Remove from the heat and stir in the vanilla. Set aside to cool.

3. Make the bottom layer: Put the flour, granola, baking soda, salt, and brown sugar in the bowl of a food processor and process briefly to combine. Add the butter and process just until the mixture is crumbly, scraping down the bowl several times. Firmly pat three quarters of the flour mixture evenly into the ungreased baking pan.

4. Spread the cooled filling evenly over the bottom layer. Sprinkle the remaining flour mixture over the filling.

5. Bake for 26 to 30 minutes, until the topping is lightly browned and firm to the touch. Place the pan on a wire rack to cool completely. Run a sharp knife around the edge of the pan, then cut into 32 bars (4 bars by 8 bars).

11 More Hints for Great Bar Cookies

1. Most bar cookies should be allowed to cool completely in the pan. Don't try to cut them while they are hot or warm—the edges will tear or crumble.

2. If you want to dress up your bars or squares a bit, do it *before* you cut them: Sprinkle with a little confectioners' sugar or cocoa sifted through a fine strainer.

3. Before cutting into individual bars or squares, carefully run a sharp knife around the edge of the pan to loosen the dough.

4. Use a sharp—not serrated—knife for cutting the baked dough into bars or squares; depending on the texture or stickiness of the cookies, you may need to wipe off the knife blade between cuts.

5. For bars spread with glaze or sticky topping, heating the knife blade makes for easier cutting. Simply hold the knife under hot water, dry off, and cut.

6. Each recipe tells you how many bars or squares to cut and how to cut them, but if you prefer to cut them larger or smaller, feel free to do so.

7. If you like, cut the cookies and, instead of removing them, store them right in the pan. Be sure to cover them tightly with plastic wrap.

8. When you remove bars or squares from the pan, lift out the corner cookie first and work from there, using a small offset spatula.

9. Store bars and squares only when completely cooled; see page 3 for advice on cookie storage.
10. Most bars and squares in this book can be frozen, so eat as many as you like and freeze the rest for another time. See page 73 for more information on freezing.
11. Wrap and bag individual bars (or packets of two or three bars) for lunchboxes, movie snacks, travel snacks.

Oatmeal Bars with Chocolate-Covered Raisins

MAKES 20 BARS

Here's an easy way to get both chocolate and raisins in a bar with a light oatmeal flavor—just add chocolate-covered raisins to the simple batter.

¾ cup flour
½ cup quick (1-minute) oatmeal, uncooked
¼ teaspoon salt
½ cup (1 stick) unsalted butter, at room temperature
½ cup packed light brown sugar
1 egg
1 egg yolk
1 teaspoon vanilla extract
¾ cup chocolate-covered raisins

1. Preheat the oven to 375°F; grease a 9 × 13-inch baking pan. In a small bowl, stir or whisk together the flour, oatmeal, and salt.

2. In a large bowl, cream the butter and brown sugar. Add the egg, egg yolk, and vanilla and beat well. Gradually add the flour mixture, blending well after each addition. Stir in the chocolate-covered raisins.

3. Pat the dough evenly into the prepared pan.

4. Bake for 18 to 22 minutes, until the top is light brown and firm to the touch and the edges are brown. Let the pan cool completely on a wire rack. Run a sharp knife around the edge of the pan, then cut into 20 bars (4 bars by 5 bars).

Almond-Cinnamon Bars

MAKES 32 BARS

This is an unusual and elegant bar cookie, very thin and crisp, buttery and spicy, with the grainy texture of finely chopped almonds. Serve with afternoon tea or at the end of a hearty dinner, with seasonal fruit.

1¼ cups flour
¼ teaspoon salt
½ cup sliced almonds (raw or toasted; with or without skins)
½ cup sugar
1 teaspoon cinnamon
½ cup (1 stick) cold unsalted butter, cut into pats
1 egg yolk
½ teaspoon almond extract

1. Preheat the oven to 350°F; grease and flour a 9 × 13-inch baking pan.
2. Put the flour, salt, almonds, sugar, and cinnamon in the bowl of a food processor and process until the almonds are coarsely ground. Add the butter and process just until the mixture is crumbly. Add the egg yolk and almond extract and process again, scraping down the bowl several times, until evenly blended.
3. Press the dough firmly and evenly into the prepared pan.
4. Bake for 22 to 24 minutes, until lightly browned. Let the pan cool on a wire rack until *warm*. Run a sharp knife around the edge of the pan. Cut into 32 bars (4 bars by 8 bars), but do not remove the cookies from the pan. Allow to cool completely, then remove carefully.

Maple-Walnut Squares

MAKES 24 SQUARES

A combination of maple syrup and crunchy toasted walnuts makes a perfect topping for these squares. Serve with apple cider for a hearty after-school snack.

For the bottom layer:
- 1½ cups flour
- ¼ teaspoon salt
- 2 tablespoons packed light brown sugar
- ½ cup (1 stick) cold unsalted butter, cut into pats

For the topping:
- 2 eggs
- ½ cup packed light brown sugar
- ½ cup maple syrup
- 1 teaspoon vanilla extract
- 1 cup coarsely chopped toasted walnuts

1. Preheat the oven to 350°F; grease a 9 × 13-inch baking pan.
2. Make the bottom layer: Put the flour, salt, and brown sugar in the bowl of a food processor and process to combine. Add the butter and process until the mixture begins to clump, scraping down the bowl several times. With moistened fingers, pat the dough evenly over the bottom of the prepared pan. Bake for 12 minutes, until dry-looking and firm to the touch. Place the pan on a wire rack to cool.

3. Make the topping: Put the eggs, brown sugar, maple syrup, and vanilla in the food processor bowl (there is no need to wash the bowl after making the bottom layer) and process until well blended. Add the walnuts and pulse several times to combine and to chop the walnuts into pea-size pieces; do not over-process or the walnut pieces will be too small. Pour the topping over the cooled dough in the pan.

4. Bake for 18 to 22 minutes, until the topping is set, crisp, and brown. Let the pan cool completely on a wire rack. Run a sharp knife around the edge of the pan, then cut into 24 squares (4 squares by 6 squares).

Honey-Almond Strips

MAKES 25 BARS

Another of my favorites—a layer of cookie dough, rich and almondy, with a deliciously sticky, buttery, sliced-almond topping flavored with real lemon juice and honey. Very pretty, too, because the almond topping gets beautifully browned during baking.

For the bottom layer:
1¾ cups flour
½ teaspoon salt
½ cup packed light brown sugar
½ cup (1 stick) cold unsalted butter, cut into pats
1 egg beaten with 1 teaspoon almond extract

For the topping:
6 tablespoons unsalted butter
¼ cup sugar
1 tablespoon fresh lemon juice
2 tablespoons honey
1 teaspoon almond extract
1 cup sliced almonds (raw or toasted; with or without skins)

1. Preheat the oven to 350°F; grease a 9 × 13-inch baking pan.
2. Make the bottom layer: Put the flour, salt, and brown sugar in the bowl of a food processor and process to combine. Add the butter and process until the mixture looks like cornmeal. Add the beaten egg and process until the mixture

is blended and forms a ball on top of the blades, scraping down the bowl several times. With flour-dusted fingers, pat the mixture evenly into the prepared pan. Chill the pan while you make the topping.

3. Make the topping: In a small saucepan over low heat, stir together the butter, sugar, lemon juice, honey, and almond extract until melted and smooth. Remove from the heat, stir in the almonds, and allow to cool until warm. Spread the topping evenly over the unbaked dough in the pan.

4. Bake for 28 to 30 minutes, until the almonds are lightly browned. Let the pan cool completely on a wire rack. Run a sharp knife around the edge of the pan, then cut into 25 bars (5 bars by 5 bars).

Currant Squares

These squares are a little like wonderful muffins or scones—try serving them warm for breakfast. They're not too rich since they're made without butter, but they're very flavorful, with plenty of currants and nuts. Great for people who don't want to eat dairy products.

1¾ cups flour
1 teaspoon baking soda
¼ teaspoon salt
1 cup currants
1 cup water
½ cup neutral vegetable oil (corn, safflower, canola, or sunflower)
1 cup sugar
1 egg
1 teaspoon vanilla extract
½ cup chopped pecans or walnuts
Confectioners' sugar

1. Preheat the oven to 375°F; grease and flour a 9 × 13-inch baking pan. In a medium-size bowl, stir or whisk together the flour, baking soda, and salt. In a small saucepan, combine the currants and water and bring to a boil; remove from the heat and allow to cool; do not drain the water from the currants.

2. In a large bowl, combine the oil, sugar, egg, and vanilla and beat well. Add the cooled currant mixture and stir well. Gradually add the flour mixture, stirring and blending well after each addition. Stir in the chopped nuts.

3. Spread the batter evenly in the prepared pan.

4. Bake for 22 to 24 minutes, until the top is very brown and a toothpick inserted in the center of the pan comes out almost clean. Let the pan cool on a wire rack until warm, then sprinkle with confectioners' sugar sifted through a fine strainer. Let the pan cool completely on a wire rack. Run a sharp knife around the edge of the pan, then cut into 24 squares (4 squares by 6 squares).

Hot Tips: Dried Fruit

You'll find a great variety of dried fruit in the ingredients lists of these bar cookie recipes—raisins, currants, prunes, dates, apricots, cherries, and others. Remember:

- Never use old, hard dried fruit in baking because it won't soften during the baking process.
- If necessary, restore dried fruit to softness by soaking it briefly in hot or boiling water just until tender. Drain, pat dry on paper towels, and then let it air-dry completely.

Ginger-Molasses Bars

Dark, rich, spicy bars—rather like gingerbread—with a firm, cakelike texture, and plenty of raisins and chopped candied ginger (if you choose it) to add interest.

1½ cups flour
½ teaspoon baking soda
¼ teaspoon salt
2 teaspoons ground ginger
½ teaspoon cinnamon
¼ teaspoon ground cloves
½ cup (1 stick) unsalted butter, at room temperature
½ cup packed dark brown sugar

½ cup unsulphured molasses (not blackstrap)
1 egg
⅓ cup water
½ cup dark raisins
¼ cup finely chopped candied ginger (optional)
Confectioners' sugar

1. Preheat the oven to 350°F; grease and flour a 9 × 13-inch baking pan. In a small bowl, stir or whisk together the flour, baking soda, salt, and spices.
2. In a large bowl, cream the butter and brown sugar. Add the molasses and the egg and beat well. Add the flour mixture alternately with the water, in three parts, blending well after each addition. Stir in the raisins and chopped candied ginger (if you are using it).
3. Spread the batter evenly in the prepared pan.
4. Bake for 18 to 22 minutes, until the top is a rich dark brown and a toothpick inserted in the center of the pan comes out clean. Let the pan cool completely on a wire rack, then sprinkle with confectioners' sugar sifted through a fine strainer. Run a sharp knife around the edge of the pan, then cut into 32 bars (4 bars by 8 bars).

Chewy Fruit and Nut Squares

MAKES 24 SQUARES

You'll love the light orange flavor of these squares. They're best when you make them with a variety of dried fruit, such as apples, prunes, apricots, and pears.

2¼ cups flour
1 teaspoon baking powder
½ teaspoon baking soda
½ teaspoon salt
½ cup light or dark raisins
1 cup chopped dried fruit: apricots, peaches, prunes, apples, pears, or any combination
¾ cup chopped walnuts or pecans

½ cup (1 stick) unsalted butter, at room temperature
½ cup sugar
½ cup packed light brown sugar
1 egg
1 teaspoon grated orange rind
¼ cup orange juice
1 teaspoon vanilla extract

1. Preheat the oven to 375°F; grease a 9 × 13-inch baking pan. In a medium-size bowl, stir or whisk together the flour, baking powder, baking soda, and salt. Add the raisins, dried fruit, and nuts and stir again, breaking up any clumps of fruit.

2. In a large bowl, cream the butter, sugar, and brown sugar. Add the egg, grated orange rind, orange juice, and vanilla and beat well. Gradually add the flour mixture, blending well after each addition.

3. Spread the batter evenly in the prepared pan.

4. Bake for 18 to 22 minutes, until the edges are browned and a toothpick inserted in the center of the pan comes out clean. Let the pan cool completely on a wire rack. Run a sharp knife around the edge of the pan, then cut into 24 squares (4 squares by 6 squares).

Hermit Bars

Traditional hermit drop cookies always include a generous amount of dried fruits and nuts, and are usually sweetened with molasses and dark brown sugar. These spicy, cakelike bars are an easy-to-make variation, full of dark raisins and chopped walnuts, with more walnuts on top.

1¾ cups flour
½ teaspoon baking soda
1 teaspoon cinnamon
½ teaspoon ground nutmeg
¼ teaspoon ground cloves
¼ teaspoon ground allspice
½ teaspoon salt
½ cup (1 stick) unsalted butter, at room temperature
⅔ cup packed dark brown sugar
1 egg
¼ cup unsulphured molasses (not blackstrap)
½ cup dark raisins
1 cup chopped walnuts

1. Preheat the oven to 350°F; grease and flour a 9 × 13-inch baking pan. In a medium-size bowl, stir or whisk together the flour, baking soda, spices, and salt.
2. In a large bowl, cream the butter and brown sugar. Add the egg and molasses and beat well. Gradually add the flour mixture, blending well after each addition. Stir in the raisins and half of the walnuts.
3. Spread the batter evenly in the prepared pan.

4. Sprinkle the top evenly with the remaining walnuts and press them lightly into the batter.

5. Bake for 18 to 20 minutes, until a toothpick inserted in the center of the pan comes out clean. Let the pan cool completely on a wire rack. Run a sharp knife around the edge of the pan, then cut into 32 bars (4 bars by 8 bars).

Hot Tips: Spices

In bar cookies, the ground spices you'll use most often are cinnamon, ginger, nutmeg, allspice, and cloves, and it's important that they be fresh and aromatic, not stale or musty.

Since ground spices tend to lose their punch rather quickly, it's smart to buy them in small quantities. Keep them in airtight containers, store them in a cool, dark place, and discard the leftovers after about six months.

Here's a tip: If you hate the thought of investing in a whole container of spice when you'll only need half, share the cost with a friend. Divide the spice into two small jars—you'll each save money, and you'll have the amount you really need.

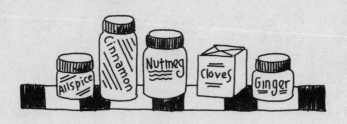

Trail Bars

Quick energy in a thick, chunky bar—each one is practically a meal in itself. Note that there are no dairy products in this recipe.

1½ cups flour
1½ cups raisin bran cereal
¾ cup quick (1-minute) oatmeal, uncooked
1 teaspoon baking soda
½ teaspoon baking powder
¼ teaspoon salt
¾ cup (1½ sticks) salted margarine, at room temperature
¾ cup sugar
½ cup light brown sugar
2 eggs
1 teaspoon vanilla extract
½ cup sweetened shredded coconut
1 cup semisweet chocolate chips
1 cup chopped, roasted, unsalted peanuts

1. Preheat the oven to 350°F; grease a 9 × 13-inch baking pan. In a medium-size bowl, stir together the flour, cereal, oatmeal, baking soda, baking powder, and salt.

2. In a large bowl, cream the margarine, sugar, and brown sugar. Add the eggs and vanilla and beat well. Gradually stir in the flour mixture, blending well after each addition. Stir in all the coconut, half of the chocolate chips, and ¾ cup of the peanuts.

3. Spread the batter evenly in the prepared pan. Sprinkle the top evenly with the remaining chocolate chips and peanuts, and press them down lightly so they are embedded in the batter.

4. Bake for 23 to 27 minutes, until the top is lightly browned and a toothpick inserted in the center of the pan comes out clean. Allow the pan to cool completely on a wire rack. Run a sharp knife around the edge of the pan, then cut into 21 bars (3 bars by 7 bars).

Hot Tips: Freezing Your Cookies

Most bar cookies freeze well in zip-lock bags or in airtight plastic containers.

- First wrap bars snugly in plastic wrap, either in one layer or in two or more layers separated by small pieces of plastic wrap; you might find it useful to wrap the cookies in packages of two, four, eight, or another convenient amount.
- After wrapping bars in plastic, seal them in a zip-lock bag or plastic container.
- To defrost, spread bars in a single layer on a wire rack and let them come to room temperature.

No-Bake Squares with Chocolate–Peanut Butter Glaze

MAKES 25 SQUARES

When it's too hot to turn on the oven, make these glazed squares that require only minimal cooking on a burner. Keep them cool in the refrigerator until the moment you eat them.

¾ cup (1½ sticks) unsalted butter
1 cup sugar
2 eggs, beaten
1 teaspoon vanilla extract
2½ cups graham cracker crumbs
1 cup semisweet chocolate chips
¼ cup smooth or crunchy peanut butter
¼ cup chopped, unsalted, roasted peanuts

1. Grease a 9 × 9-inch baking pan.
2. In a large saucepan over low heat, melt the butter; remove the pan from the heat. Add the sugar and stir well. Add the eggs, stir well, and return to medium-low heat. Cook, stirring constantly, until the mixture begins to bubble. Continue cooking and stirring for about 5 minutes longer, until thickened. Allow the mixture to cool. Stir in the vanilla, then the graham cracker crumbs.
3. Spread the mixture evenly in the prepared pan.
4. Refrigerate for 30 minutes, or until firm.
5. In a small saucepan, melt and stir the chocolate chips and peanut butter until blended, to make a glaze. Spread the glaze evenly on the chilled dough in

the pan. Sprinkle with the chopped peanuts. Return the pan to the refrigerator until firm. Using a sharp knife dipped in hot water, cut into 25 squares (5 squares by 5 squares), wiping the knife blade between cuts. The hotter the knife, the easier the cutting will be. Refrigerate the cookies until needed.

Simple Decorations for Bar Cookies

These decorations are applied to the top of the cookie dough *after* baking but *before* cutting into bars or squares. Be sure to choose a decoration with a flavor that is appropriate for the cookie.

- While the dough is still hot, sprinkle with miniature chocolate chips; the chips will melt slightly and adhere to the dough. When cool, cut as specified in the recipe.
- Spread vanilla or rum glaze on cooled dough; sift cocoa over the glaze.
- Spread chocolate glaze on cooled dough; sift confectioners' sugar over the glaze.
- Spread any of the glazes on pages 122 to 126 on cooled dough. Immediately, while the glaze is still tacky, sprinkle evenly with one of the following: chopped nuts; toasted coconut; colored sugar; multicolored dots; chocolate or multicolored sprinkles; chopped white or dark chocolate; miniature marshmallows.
- Prepare vanilla glaze and chocolate glaze; add enough liquid to the

chocolate glaze to allow it to pour freely from a spoon. Spread vanilla glaze on the cooled dough; let it set. Drizzle with chocolate glaze, making a crisscross pattern.

- Melt and stir twelve to fifteen vanilla or chocolate caramels with just enough milk to allow the mixture to pour freely from a spoon. Drizzle over cooled cookie dough.

Squares and Bars with Fruit

Many bar cookie recipes incorporate dried fruit (such as raisins and currants) for incidental texture and flavor. The recipes in this section are a little different since they are characterized by the dried and fresh fruit they use: fresh strawberries, raspberries, blueberries, and bananas; dried pineapple, cranberries, and prunes. They range from the simple and hearty—*Banana–Sour Cream Squares, Apple Crumb Squares*, and *Glazed Cranberry-Orange Bars*—to the elegant and festive—*Fresh Raspberry Squares with Drizzled Chocolate, Lemon-Glazed Pineapple Squares*, and *Strawberry-Custard Squares*—a recipe for every occasion.

Banana–Sour Cream Squares

MAKES 16 SQUARES

Like traditional banana cake, these squares are moist and tender, with a good flavor of bananas and crunch of nuts. The glaze gives the squares a lovely finishing touch; if you don't like rum glaze, try vanilla (page 122) or lemon (page 125).

1 cup flour
1/2 teaspoon baking soda
1/2 teaspoon salt
1/4 cup (1/2 stick) unsalted butter, at room temperature
1/2 cup sour cream
3/4 cup sugar

1 egg
1 teaspoon vanilla extract
3/4 cup mashed ripe bananas (about 1 1/2 medium bananas)
1/2 cup chopped walnuts or pecans
Rum Glaze (page 125)

1. Preheat the oven to 375°F; grease and flour a 9 × 9-inch baking pan. In a small bowl, stir or whisk together the flour, baking soda, and salt.

2. In a large bowl, cream the butter, sour cream, and sugar. Add the egg, vanilla, and mashed bananas and beat again. Gradually add the flour mixture, blending well after each addition. Stir in the nuts.

3. Spread the batter evenly in the prepared pan.

4. Bake for 20 to 22 minutes, until the edges are lightly browned and a toothpick inserted in the center of the pan comes out clean. Let the pan cool completely on a wire rack. Spread glaze evenly over the top and allow to set at room temperature or in the refrigerator. Run a sharp knife around the edge of the pan, then cut into 16 squares (4 squares by 4 squares), wiping the knife blade between cuts.

Hot Tips: Sugar and Other Sweeteners

Sweeteners are *not* interchangeable in cookie baking, so it's important to use the sweetener listed in the recipe.

- **Sugar:** Ordinary white granulated sugar; generic or inexpensive sugar tends to be coarse (making it difficult to cream sugar with butter), so choose a premium brand.
- **Light or dark brown sugar:** Granulated sugar blended with molasses; should be moist and clumpy; pack it so firmly into your measuring cup that it holds the shape of the cup when turned out.
- **Superfine sugar:** Finely ground granulated sugar that dissolves very easily.
- **Confectioners' sugar:** Also called powdered or 10X sugar; used mostly in glazes and frostings; usually contains a little cornstarch, which gives it a slight undertaste that is counteracted by stronger flavors such as vanilla or chocolate.
- **Honey:** Adds flavor (depending on the type of honey used) and moistness to cookies; don't be tempted to substitute honey for sugar in baking.
- **Molasses:** Use dark, unsulphured molasses for the best flavor; avoid blackstrap molasses (too strong) and light molasses (too mild).
- **Light corn syrup:** Makes cookies moist and chewy, since it prevents other sugars from crystallizing.

Apple Crumb Squares

Thick, spicy applesauce is the filling for these hearty, substantial squares that have a cookie bottom and a generous crumb topping. One of these goodies, with a cup of coffee or a glass of milk, will hold the hungriest snacker until dinnertime.

For the bottom layer:
2 cups flour
1 teaspoon baking powder
½ teaspoon salt
6 tablespoons unsalted butter, at room temperature
¾ cup packed light brown sugar
1 egg

For the filling:
2 cups applesauce
1 teaspoon fresh lemon juice
¼ teaspoon cinnamon
Dash of nutmeg

For the topping:
¾ cup flour
½ cup sugar
Pinch of salt
6 tablespoons cold unsalted butter, cut into pats
¼ cup chopped walnuts

1. Preheat the oven to 350°F; grease a 9 × 9-inch baking pan.

2. Make the bottom layer: In a medium-size bowl, stir or whisk together the flour, baking powder, and salt. In a large bowl, cream the butter and brown sugar. Add the egg and beat well. Gradually add the flour mixture, blending well after each addition. With flour-dusted fingers, pat the dough evenly into the prepared pan, pressing it about ¼ inch up the sides.

3. Make the filling: Put all the filling ingredients in a large skillet and simmer over medium-low heat, stirring often, until reduced by half. Let the filling cool.

4. Make the topping: Put the flour, sugar, and salt in the bowl of a food processor and process to combine. Add the butter and process just until the mixture is crumbly. Add the walnuts and pulse several times to combine; do not overprocess or the walnut pieces will be too small.

5. Spread the cooled filling evenly over the dough in the pan. Sprinkle the topping evenly over the filling; it will make an almost solid layer.

6. Bake for 30 to 34 minutes, until the topping is lightly browned. Let the pan cool completely on a wire rack. Run a sharp knife around the edge of the pan, then cut into 16 squares (4 squares by 4 squares).

Pear-Almond Squares

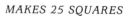

MAKES 25 SQUARES

If you like fruit betties and crumbles, these bars, with their succulent pear topping over an egg-rich cookie layer, will please you, too.

Tip: In this recipe it's important to use pears that are not too ripe; the pears should be quite firm so they don't give off too much juice during baking.

For the bottom layer:
1¾ cups flour
6 tablespoons sugar
⅛ teaspoon salt
½ cup (1 stick) cold unsalted butter, cut into pats
3 egg yolks beaten with ½ teaspoon almond extract

For the topping:
2 firm-ripe Bosc, Anjou, or Bartlett pears (¾ to 1 pound)
½ cup sugar
½ cup finely chopped toasted almonds (with or without skins)
½ teaspoon vanilla extract
Pinch of salt
2 tablespoons unsalted butter

1. Preheat the oven to 350°F; grease a 9 × 9-inch baking pan.
2. Make the bottom layer: Put the flour, sugar, and salt in the bowl of a food processor and pulse to combine. Add the butter and process until the mixture looks like coarse meal. Add the beaten egg yolks and process until the mixture

begins to clump, scraping down the bowl several times. With moistened fingers, pat the dough evenly into the prepared pan, pressing it about ¼ inch up the sides.

3. Make the topping: Peel, quarter, and core the pears, making sure to remove all the seeds and hard matter; chop the pears into pea-size pieces. Put the pears, sugar, almonds, vanilla, salt, and butter in a saucepan over low heat and stir until the butter melts and coats the pears. Let the topping cool until warm, then spread it evenly over the unbaked dough in the pan.

4. Bake for 33 to 37 minutes, until the edges of the dough are browned; the pears will still be firm and the topping will look rather juicy. Allow the pan to cool completely on a wire rack. Run a sharp knife around the edge of the pan, then cut into 25 squares (5 squares by 5 squares). Keep the bars refrigerated until half an hour before serving.

Hot Tips: Whipped Cream

To turn a simple bar cookie into a fancy one or a fancy one into a mad indulgence, add a dollop of whipped cream.

- Heavy cream doubles in volume when you whip it, so decide how much *whipped* cream you want and divide that amount in half— that's how much *liquid* heavy cream you should start with: ½ cup liquid cream to make 1 cup whipped cream; ¾ cup liquid cream to make 1½ cups whipped.
- To make lightly sweetened whipped cream, add 1 tablespoon confectioners' sugar per each ½ cup liquid cream, before whipping. Put the cream and sugar in a deep bowl; beat at low speed until the cream forms soft mounds when dropped from a spoon. If you like, continue beating until the cream is stiff, but be careful not to overbeat or the cream may turn to butter.
- For a tasty variation, make flavored sweetened whipped cream by adding a little vanilla or almond extract to the heavy cream before whipping.

- To garnish the dollops of whipped cream, top with any of the following: a dusting of nutmeg or cocoa powder; a few chocolate or multicolored sprinkles; colored dots; grated or shaved chocolate; miniature chocolate chips; chopped pistachios.

Glazed Cranberry-Orange Bars

Here's a cakelike bar cookie with a favorite flavor combination: the rich sweetness of orange marmalade and the zing of tart dried cranberries. The glaze adds a special touch, but if you're in a hurry, feel free to omit it.

1½ cups flour
1 teaspoon baking powder
½ teaspoon salt
1 cup (about 6 ounces) dried cranberries
6 tablespoons unsalted butter, at room temperature
¾ cup sugar
¾ cup orange marmalade
2 eggs
Vanilla Glaze (page 122) or Lemon Glaze (page 125)

1. Preheat the oven to 350°F; grease a 9 × 13-inch baking pan. In a small bowl, stir or whisk together the flour, baking powder, and salt. Put the dried cranberries in a small saucepan with water to cover; bring to a simmer and continue simmering for about 5 minutes, until the cranberries are soft. Drain and pat dry on paper towels.

2. In a large bowl, cream the butter and sugar. Add the marmalade and eggs and beat well. Gradually add the flour mixture, blending well after each addition. Stir in the cranberries.

3. Spread the batter evenly in the prepared pan.

4. Bake for 26 to 30 minutes, until the top is golden brown and a toothpick inserted in the center of the pan comes out clean. Let the pan cool completely

on a wire rack. Spread glaze evenly over the baked layer in the pan and allow to set at room temperature or in the refrigerator. Run a sharp knife around the edge of the pan, then cut into 32 bars (4 bars by 8 bars), wiping the knife blade between cuts.

Hot Tips: Grated Lemon or Orange Rind

Grated lemon or orange rind (sometimes called *zest*) adds to cookies a wonderfully intense flavor that can't be duplicated with any other ingredient. Here's how to make it:

- Use a box grater (which will stand firmly on your kitchen counter) placed on a piece of waxed paper.
- Rub the skin of the lemon or orange over the grater in small circles, pressing firmly. Move to a new spot as soon as the white layer under the yellow or orange skin is exposed.
- Stop occasionally and use a small, stiff pastry brush to remove the bits of rind clinging to the grater and to clear the holes: Brush down and diagonally and inside the grater. Tap the grater on the counter to loosen additional bits of rind.
- When you've finished grating the whole lemon or orange, brush the grater again. Use the flat edge of a spatula or knife to gather all the bits of rind, and measure by lightly packing the grated rind into a measuring spoon.

Strawberry-Custard Squares

Each square is topped with a thick slice of fresh strawberry—the tartness of the strawberry is a perfect counterpoint to the sweetness of the crisp cookie base and the richness of the custard filling.

For the bottom layer:
½ cup (1 stick) unsalted butter, at room temperature
½ cup packed light brown sugar
1⅓ cups flour stirred with ¼ teaspoon salt

For the filling:
1 cup sour cream
1 egg
¼ cup sugar
½ teaspoon baking soda

For the topping:
7 medium-large strawberries, hulled
Confectioners' sugar

1. Preheat the oven to 350°F; grease a 9 × 9-inch baking pan.
2. Make the bottom layer: In a large bowl, cream the butter and brown sugar. Gradually add the flour, blending well after each addition. With moistened fingers, pat the dough evenly into the prepared pan. Bake for 15 minutes, until dry-looking and lightly browned. Let the pan cool on a wire rack until warm.
3. Make the filling: In the same large bowl (no need to wash it), beat the sour

cream, egg, sugar, and baking soda until well blended. Spread the filling over the warm dough in the pan. Bake for 15 to 16 minutes longer, until the custard is set.

4. With the tip of a knife, mark the top in 25 squares (5 squares by 5 squares); do not cut yet.

5. Make the topping: Cut each strawberry into 4 slices, top to bottom. Place 1 slice on each marked square; there will be 3 slices left over. Sprinkle with confectioners' sugar sifted through a fine strainer. When completely cool, run a sharp knife around the edge of the pan, then cut the squares apart along the marked lines.

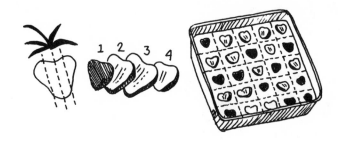

Fresh Raspberry Squares with Drizzled Chocolate

Elegant and special enough for the fanciest dinner party, but simple to prepare. Fresh raspberries are arranged on a cookie crust that has been painted with currant jelly, and the berries are topped with a generous drizzle of melted semisweet chocolate.

1 ½ cups flour
⅛ teaspoon salt
6 tablespoons sugar
½ cup (1 stick) cold unsalted butter, cut into pats
1 egg yolk beaten with 2 tablespoons heavy cream or milk
½ cup currant jelly
80 fresh raspberries
4 ounces high-quality semisweet chocolate (such as Callebaut, Lindt, Valrhona, or Ghirardelli), chopped
¼ cup heavy cream or milk

1. Preheat the oven to 375°F; grease a 9 × 9-inch baking pan.
2. Put the flour, salt, and sugar in the bowl of a food processor and pulse several times to combine. Add the butter and process until the mixture is like coarse meal. Add the yolk mixture and process until all the dough forms clumps, scraping down the bowl several times. Pat the dough evenly over the bottom of the prepared pan. Bake for 20 minutes, until golden on top and brown at the edges. Let the pan cool on a wire rack until warm.

3. In a small saucepan over low heat, melt the currant jelly, stirring constantly until smooth. Using a soft pastry brush, spread the melted jelly evenly over the warm crust in the pan.

4. With the tip of a sharp knife, mark the dough in 16 squares (4 squares by 4 squares); do not cut yet. Arrange 5 raspberries on each square, as shown.

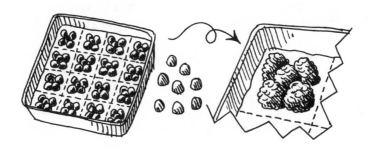

5. In a small saucepan over very low heat, stir the semisweet chocolate and cream (or milk) until melted and smooth. Using a spoon or a small whisk, drizzle the chocolate mixture over the raspberries. Let the chocolate set at room temperature or in the refrigerator. Run a sharp knife around the edge of the pan, then cut the squares apart along the marked lines.

Blueberry Bars with Lattice Top

This pan of bars consists of a bottom layer of tender cookie dough and a sweet blueberry filling, topped with a lattice of dough strips. The dough is rather fragile to work with, so making the lattice top takes a little skill.

For the bottom layer and lattice top:
2½ cups flour
½ teaspoon baking powder
½ teaspoon salt
1 cup (2 sticks) unsalted butter, at room temperature
½ cup sugar
1 egg

For the filling:
3 cups fresh or frozen blueberries
½ cup sugar

1. Grease a 9 × 13-inch baking pan.

2. Make the bottom layer: In a medium-size bowl, stir or whisk together the flour, baking powder, and salt. In a large bowl, cream the butter and sugar. Add the egg and beat well. Gradually add the flour mixture, blending well after each addition. Reserve a quarter of the dough and wrap snugly in plastic. Pat the remaining three quarters of the dough evenly into the prepared pan, pressing it ¼ inch up the sides. Refrigerate the wrapped dough and the pan of dough for 30 minutes.

3. Make the filling: In a medium-size saucepan over low heat, combine the

blueberries and sugar and simmer, stirring often, until the mixture is as thick as jam, about 30 minutes. Remove from the heat and allow to cool until warm.

4. Preheat the oven to 375°F. Spread the warm filling over the chilled dough in the pan. On a lightly floured surface, roll out the reserved dough to ⅛ inch thick; cut into ½-inch-wide strips. Crisscross the strips over the filling, patching strips together when necessary, to make a lattice top as shown; the strips will be a bit fragile, so work carefully.

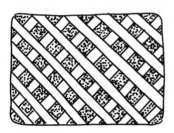

5. Bake for 25 to 30 minutes, until the lattice is lightly browned. Let the pan cool completely on a wire rack. Run a sharp knife around the edge of the pan, then cut into 20 bars (4 bars by 5 bars).

Prune-Filled Squares

Yummy prune filling, flavored with orange rind and almond extract, is sandwiched between an oatmeal-cinnamon cookie layer and a walnut-crumb topping in these snackable squares.

For the filling:
¾ cup pitted prunes
6 tablespoons water
1½ tablespoons sugar
½ teaspoon grated orange rind
¼ teaspoon almond extract

For the bottom layer and topping:
1 cup flour
1 cup quick (1-minute) oatmeal, uncooked
½ cup packed light brown sugar
½ teaspoon cinnamon
¼ teaspoon salt
10 tablespoons cold unsalted butter, cut into pats
½ cup chopped walnuts

1. Make the filling: Put the prunes, water, and sugar in a heavy saucepan and simmer, partially covered, until the prunes are soft and the water is almost gone, 8 to 10 minutes. Put the prune mixture in the bowl of a food processor with the grated orange rind and almond extract and process until smooth. Transfer to a small bowl and set aside to cool. Wash the food processor bowl.

2. Preheat the oven to 350°F; grease a 9 × 9-inch baking pan.

3. Make the bottom layer: Put the flour, oatmeal, brown sugar, cinnamon, and salt in the food processor bowl and pulse several times to combine. Add the butter and process until the mixture clumps, scraping down the bowl several times. Remove two thirds of the mixture from the processor and press it evenly into the prepared pan.

4. Make the topping: Add the chopped walnuts to the remaining mixture in the food processor and pulse several times to combine; do not overprocess or the walnut pieces will be too small.

5. Spread the prune filling evenly over the unbaked layer in the pan. Sprinkle the topping evenly over the filling and press it down lightly.

6. Bake for 28 to 32 minutes, until the top is browned. Let the pan cool completely on a wire rack. Run a sharp knife around the edge of the pan, then cut into 25 squares (5 squares by 5 squares).

Lemon-Glazed Pineapple Squares

MAKES 25 SQUARES

These squares feature bright, sunny flavors—pineapple and grated lemon rind, with a finish of tangy lemon glaze. If you like, sprinkle ¼ cup toasted coconut on the glaze before it dries, pressing the coconut lightly into the glaze.

1 cup flour
½ teaspoon baking powder
¼ teaspoon salt
½ teaspoon grated lemon rind
½ cup (1 stick) unsalted butter, at room temperature
¾ cup packed light brown sugar

1 egg
1 teaspoon vanilla extract
1 cup chopped dried pineapple (about 6 ounces)
½ cup chopped macadamia nuts or pecans
Lemon Glaze (page 125)

1. Preheat the oven to 350°F; grease and flour a 9 × 9-inch baking pan. In a small bowl, stir or whisk together the flour, baking powder, salt, and lemon rind.

2. In a large bowl, cream the butter and brown sugar. Add the egg and vanilla and beat well. Gradually add the flour mixture, blending well after each addition. Stir in the chopped pineapple and chopped nuts.

3. Spread the batter evenly in the prepared pan.

4. Bake for 23 to 27 minutes, until the top is golden, the edges are brown, and a toothpick inserted in the center of the pan comes out clean. Let the pan cool completely on a wire rack.

5. Spread glaze evenly over the baked layer in the pan and allow to set at room temperature or in the refrigerator. Run a sharp knife around the edge of the pan, then cut into 25 squares (5 squares by 5 squares), wiping the knife blade between cuts.

Extra-Special Squares and Bars

When you want an extra-special dessert that's totally delicious yet easy to make, one of the recipes in this section will do the trick. What makes them extra special? Luxurious ingredients (as in *White Chocolate Chunk–Macadamia Bars* and *Cappuccino Squares with Vanilla Cream Glaze*), sophisticated flavors (as in *Chocolate-Chestnut Squares* and *Florentine Bars*), and those extra touches that lift the familiar to elegant heights—as in *Pine Nut–Orange Bars* and *Gingerbread Bars with Pecan-Bourbon Topping*. Try one of these bar cookies for a grand finale to any dinner party or celebration.

Chocolate-Chestnut Squares

MAKES 25 SQUARES

This is a knockout cookie—a fabulous, thick layer of spiked chestnut filling, sweet and rich, over a moist chocolate layer. Try serving these squares at parties or on holidays, with a dusting of cocoa powder and a garnish of chocolate coffee beans.

For the bottom layer:
½ cup flour
⅓ cup cocoa powder, sifted
¼ teaspoon salt
½ cup (1 stick) unsalted butter, at room temperature
1 cup sugar
2 eggs
1 teaspoon vanilla extract

For the filling:
1 7- to 8-ounce can or jar of whole peeled roasted chestnuts (about 20 chestnuts)
¼ cup Cognac or brandy
¼ cup (½ stick) unsalted butter, at room temperature
3 ounces cream cheese, at room temperature
¾ cup confectioners' sugar

For the topping:
Cocoa powder
50 chocolate coffee beans

1. Preheat the oven to 350°F; grease and flour a 9 × 9-inch baking pan.

2. Make the bottom layer: In a small bowl, stir or whisk together the flour, cocoa, and salt. In a large bowl, cream the butter and sugar. Add the eggs and vanilla and beat well. Gradually add the flour mixture, blending well after each addition. Spread the batter evenly in the prepared pan. Bake for 23 to 27 minutes, until the top is dry and a toothpick inserted in the center of the pan comes out clean. Let the pan cool completely on a wire rack. Do not cut yet, but run a sharp knife around the edge of the pan.

3. Make the filling: Break the chestnuts into the bowl of a food processor. Add the Cognac or brandy and process until the mixture is smooth and pasty, scraping down the bowl several times. Add the butter, cream cheese, and confectioners' sugar and process until smooth, scraping down the bowl several times. If the filling is very soft, chill until it is about as firm as peanut butter.

4. Spread the filling evenly over the cooled layer in the pan. With the tip of a knife, mark the filling in 25 squares (5 squares by 5 squares).

5. Sprinkle with a little cocoa sifted through a fine strainer, and top each square with a pair of chocolate coffee beans. Cover the pan carefully and chill until the filling is very firm. Cut the squares apart along the marked lines. Keep refrigerated until serving.

Pecan-Meringue Squares

MAKES 16 SQUARES

To make these delectable squares you'll top the rich bottom layer with a sweet, sticky meringue that contains a generous amount of chopped pecans. Note that the eggs are separated—be sure you don't accidentally throw out either the yolks or the whites!

For the bottom layer:
1 1/4 cups flour
1 teaspoon baking powder
1/4 teaspoon salt
1/2 cup (1 stick) unsalted butter, at room temperature
1/2 cup packed light brown sugar
2 egg yolks

For the topping:
2 egg whites
1/2 teaspoon vanilla extract
1/2 cup packed light brown sugar
1/2 cup chopped pecans

1. Preheat the oven to 325°F; grease a 9 × 9-inch baking pan.
2. Make the bottom layer: In a small bowl, stir or whisk together the flour, baking powder, and salt. In a large bowl, cream the butter and brown sugar. Add the egg yolks and beat well. Gradually add the flour mixture, blending well after each addition. Spread the batter evenly in the prepared pan.
3. Make the topping: In a large bowl, with clean beaters, beat the egg whites

and vanilla until foamy. Beat in the brown sugar 1 tablespoon at a time and continue beating until the mixture is thick and glossy and stands in soft peaks. Gently stir in the pecans. Spread the topping over the unbaked layer in the pan.

4. Bake for 28 to 32 minutes, until the meringue topping is lightly browned and firm to the touch. Let the pan cool completely on a wire rack. Run a sharp knife around the edge of the pan, then cut carefully into 16 squares (4 squares by 4 squares), wiping the knife blade between cuts. The meringue topping is quite sticky, so be patient while you're cutting.

Cappuccino Squares with Vanilla Cream Glaze

MAKES 24 SQUARES

Do you love cocoa-dusted cappuccino? Try these intensely chocolate-and-coffee-flavored squares with a dense, fudgy texture, laced with nuts and set off by vanilla glaze.

Tip: It's important to use really good chocolate in this cookie.

6 ounces high-quality bittersweet chocolate (such as Callebaut, Lindt, Valrhona or Ghirardelli), chopped
9 tablespoons unsalted butter
2 tablespoons instant coffee granules dissolved in 1 tablespoon boiling water
1 cup plus 2 tablespoons sugar
1 1/2 teaspoons vanilla extract
3 eggs
3/4 cup flour stirred with 1/4 teaspoon salt
3/4 cup chopped walnuts or pecans (optional)
Vanilla Glaze (page 122), made with heavy cream
Cinnamon or cocoa powder (optional)

1. Preheat the oven to 350°F; grease and flour a 9 × 13-inch baking pan.
2. In a large metal bowl set over a saucepan containing 2 inches of barely simmering water, combine the chocolate, butter, and coffee mixture, stirring until melted and smooth. Remove the bowl from the saucepan and allow to cool until warm. Whisk in the sugar and vanilla, then whisk in the eggs 1 at a

time. Add the flour and *stir* just until mixed. If you are making the squares with chopped nuts, stir them into the batter.

3. Spread the batter evenly in the prepared pan.

4. Bake for 22 to 24 minutes, until the top looks dry and a toothpick inserted in the center of the pan comes out almost clean. Place the pan on a wire rack and allow to cool completely.

5. Spread the glaze evenly on the cooled layer in the pan. If you like, dust with cinnamon or with cocoa sifted through a fine strainer. Refrigerate until the glaze is firm. Run a sharp knife around the edge of the pan, then cut into 24 squares (4 squares by 6 squares), wiping the knife blade between cuts.

Have Bar, Will Travel

Many bar cookies are great travelers, so don't hesitate to send a batch to your kids at school or camp, your relatives on the coast, or your sweetheart on the other side of town.

1. Pick simple, solid bars or squares that don't require refrigeration; avoid glazed or fragile bars. Here are some good choices:

Chocolate Chip Squares (page 10)
Butterscotch Bars (page 19)
Classic Blondies (page 20)
Crunchy Peanut Butter Bars (page 32)
Fudge Fingers (page 34)
Ginger-Molasses Bars (page 68)
Chewy Fruit and Nut Squares (page 69)
Banana–Sour Cream Squares (page 80)
Glazed Cranberry-Orange Bars (page 88)

2. Choose a sturdy container with a tight-fitting lid: a stiff cardboard box, plastic kitchen container, plastic storage container, or cookie tin.

3. Line the container with plastic wrap to prevent the cookies

from absorbing any unwanted odors. Add a ½-inch layer of slightly crumpled waxed paper to the bottom of the container.

4. Arrange a layer of bars or squares on a long piece of plastic wrap, in a shape that will fit neatly into your container. Place a smaller piece of plastic wrap over the layer and make another layer of cookies; repeat for a third layer, and a fourth one, if you like. Bring the ends of the long piece of plastic wrap up and tuck them snugly around the package of cookies. (Be sure the whole package will fit into your container.) Place the package in a zip-lock bag and seal; place the zip-lock bag in your sturdy container.

5. Tuck crumpled waxed paper on all sides of the zip-lock bag. Add a layer of crumpled waxed paper on top and cover with the lid. The cookies should be snug in their nest of waxed paper.

6. If the container is strong enough (for example, a clear plastic shoebox), simply wrap it in two layers of heavy paper and tape it securely. If the container is not very strong (such as a cardboard shoebox), line a larger box with plenty of crumpled newspaper all around the container; be sure the container is "floating" in the newspaper. Top with another layer of crumpled newspaper and tape the bigger box closed.

Florentine Bars

These are festive, elegant bars that will look wonderful on your holiday table. The buttery cookie layer is spread with a colorful mixture of chopped dried cherries, pineapple, and apricots combined with sliced almonds, then drizzled with a crisscross pattern of dark chocolate glaze.

For the bottom layer:
3 cups flour
¼ teaspoon salt
¾ cup sugar
1 cup (2 sticks) cold unsalted butter, cut into pats
2 egg yolks beaten with ¼ cup heavy cream or milk

For the topping:
¼ cup (½ stick) unsalted butter
¾ cup honey
2 tablespoons heavy cream
1 cup sliced blanched almonds
½ cup chopped dried tart cherries
½ cup chopped dried apricots
½ cup chopped dried pineapple
1 tablespoon grated orange rind

For the glaze:
1 ounce unsweetened chocolate, chopped
1 tablespoon unsalted butter
3 tablespoons heavy cream
¾ cup sifted confectioners' sugar

1. Preheat the oven to 350°F; grease and flour a 10½ × 15½-inch jelly roll pan.

2. Make the bottom layer: Put the flour, salt, and sugar in the bowl of a food processor and pulse several times to combine. Add the butter and process until the mixture looks like coarse meal. Add the yolk mixture and process until all the dough forms clumps, scraping down the bowl several times. Pat the dough evenly over the bottom of the prepared pan. Bake for 20 minutes, until the top is dry and very lightly browned. Let the pan cool on a wire rack.

3. Make the topping: In a large saucepan over medium heat, melt and stir the butter, honey, and cream until blended. Boil for 1 minute, stirring constantly. Remove from the heat and stir in the almonds, cherries, apricots, pineapple, and grated orange rind.

4. Spread the topping evenly over the cooled layer in the pan.

5. Bake for 13 to 15 minutes longer, until the edges are browned. Let the pan cool completely on a wire rack.

6. Make the glaze: In a small saucepan over very low heat, stir together the chopped chocolate, butter, and cream. Whisk in the confectioners' sugar until smooth.

7. Using a spoon or a small wire whisk, drizzle the warm glaze in crisscross lines over the topping. Allow the glaze to set at room temperature or in the refrigerator. Run a sharp knife around the edge of the pan, then cut into 60 bars (6 bars by 10 bars), wiping the knife blade between cuts.

White Chocolate Chunk–Macadamia Bars

Super-chewy and buttery, chock-full of white chocolate chips and toasted macadamia nuts—one of these small bars goes a long way toward satisfying a sweet tooth. Easy to make for such a special cookie.

1 ½ cups flour
½ teaspoon baking soda
½ teaspoon salt
11 tablespoons unsalted butter, at room temperature
½ cup sugar

½ cup packed dark brown sugar
1 egg
1 teaspoon vanilla extract
¾ cup coarsely chopped, toasted, unsalted macadamia nuts
1 cup white chocolate chips

1. Preheat the oven to 325°F; grease a 9 × 13-inch baking pan. In a small bowl, stir or whisk together the flour, baking soda, and salt.
2. In a large bowl, cream the butter, sugar, and brown sugar. Add the egg and vanilla and beat well. Gradually add the flour mixture, blending well after each addition. Stir in the macadamia nuts and white chocolate chips.
3. Spread the batter evenly in the prepared pan.
4. Bake for 28 to 30 minutes, until the top is well browned and a toothpick inserted in the center of the pan comes out clean. Let the pan cool completely on a wire rack. Run a sharp knife around the edge of the pan, then cut into 32 bars (4 bars by 8 bars).

More Simple Decorations for Bar Cookies

These are decorations for individual bars or squares. Place the cookies an inch apart on a wire rack or a piece of waxed paper and apply the decoration to each cookie as described. Be sure the decoration you choose is appropriate to the cookie you're decorating.

- Put a dollop of whipped cream on each bar or square. If you like, add a couple of chocolate chips, a bit of candied ginger or candied fruit, a small candy, a sprinkling of multicolored dots, or a dusting of cocoa or nutmeg.
- Top a lemon-glazed bar or square with slivers of candied orange peel.
- Press a few white chocolate chips or a little chopped white chocolate onto any chocolate-glazed bar or square.
- Top glazed bars with fresh fruit: whole blueberries or raspberries; sliced strawberries; sliced peaches, nectarines or plums; sliced bananas.
- Pipe a rosette of frosting on each bar or square; top with anything from a small chocolate candy to a crystallized violet.

Viennese Hazelnut Bars

Moist, tender bars, rich in hazelnuts, with a thin layer of butterscotch glaze and a pretty sprinkling of additional hazelnuts.

2 cups flour
2 teaspoons baking powder
½ teaspoon salt
½ teaspoon cinnamon
1 cup (2 sticks) unsalted butter, at room temperature

1 cup packed light brown sugar
2 eggs
1 teaspoon vanilla extract
1 cup chopped skinned hazelnuts, toasted
Butterscotch Glaze (page 126)

1. Preheat the oven to 350°F; grease a 10½ × 15½-inch jelly roll pan. In a medium-size bowl, stir or whisk together the flour, baking powder, salt, and cinnamon.
2. In a large bowl, cream the butter and brown sugar. Add the eggs and vanilla and beat well. Gradually add the flour mixture, blending well after each addition. Stir in half of the hazelnuts.
3. Spread the dough evenly in the prepared pan.
4. Bake for 18 to 22 minutes, until the top is lightly browned and a toothpick inserted in the center of the pan comes out clean. Let the pan cool on a wire rack until warm.
5. Use a spatula to spread the glaze evenly over the warm layer in the pan. Immediately sprinkle with the remaining hazelnuts and pat them lightly into the glaze. Allow the glaze to set at room temperature or in the refrigerator. Run a sharp knife around the edge of the pan, then cut into 32 bars (4 bars by 8 bars).

How to Toast Nuts

Spread whole or chopped nuts—almonds, hazelnuts, walnuts, pecans, or macadamias—on a jelly roll pan or other pan with sides (nuts tend to slide off a baking sheet) and place in a preheated 350°F oven for 5 to 10 minutes. When the nuts smell toasty and a *cooled* nut is crisp and crunchy, the nuts are ready. (Keep in mind that chopped nuts toast more quickly than whole nuts.) Be sure to watch carefully to avoid burning. Let the nuts cool in the pan on a wire rack.

Tip: To remove the papery skins of toasted hazelnuts (as much as will come off), rub a few hazelnuts at a time between your palms or in a rough dish towel.

Tip: If almonds must be blanched (skinned) before toasting, put them in a pot of boiling water for a minute or so, then drain and rinse in cold water; pinch the brown skins off.

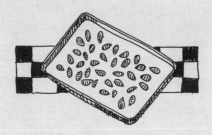

Coconut-Almond Squares

The surface of these squares becomes brown and temptingly crisp during baking, while the sweet filling of coconut and almonds stays chewy and soft over a tender cookie layer.

For the bottom layer:
1 1/2 cups flour
1/4 teaspoon salt
2 tablespoons packed light brown sugar
1/2 cup (1 stick) cold unsalted butter, cut into pats

For the topping:
3 tablespoons flour
1/2 teaspoon salt
1 cup packed light brown sugar
1 1/2 cups sweetened shredded coconut
1 cup chopped blanched almonds, toasted
2 eggs, beaten
1 teaspoon vanilla extract

1. Preheat the oven to 350°F; grease a 9 × 13-inch baking pan.
2. Make the bottom layer: Put the flour, salt, and brown sugar in the bowl of a food processor and pulse to combine. Add the butter and process until the mixture clumps, scraping down the bowl several times. With moistened fingers, pat the dough evenly over the bottom of the prepared pan. Bake for 12

minutes, until dry-looking and firm to the touch. Place the pan on a wire rack to cool.

3. Make the topping: In a large bowl, stir together the flour, salt, brown sugar, coconut, and almonds. Add the beaten eggs and vanilla and blend well.

4. Spread the topping evenly over the cooled layer in the pan.

5. Bake for 23 to 27 minutes, until the filling is lightly browned and set. Let the pan cool completely on a wire rack. Run a sharp knife around the edge of the pan, then cut into 24 squares (4 squares by 6 squares).

Linzer Squares

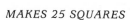

You're probably familiar with traditional linzertorte, a buttery crust topped with raspberry jam and an elegant lattice of dough strips. These squares are an easy variation—there's no lattice top, so there's no rolling and cutting the dough. Simply spread the dough with jam and sprinkle with reserved topping.

1 cup walnuts
1½ cups flour
¾ teaspoon baking powder
½ teaspoon cinnamon
¼ teaspoon salt
¼ cup sugar

½ cup packed light brown sugar
½ cup (1 stick) cold unsalted butter,
    cut into pats
1 egg, lightly beaten
¾ cup seedless raspberry jam

1. Preheat the oven to 375°F; grease a 9 × 9-inch baking pan.
2. Put the walnuts in the bowl of a food processor and grind. Add the flour, baking powder, cinnamon, salt, sugar, and brown sugar and process to combine. Add the butter and process until the mixture is like small crumbs. Reserve ½ cup of the mixture and set aside. Add the beaten egg to the processor bowl and process just until the mixture begins to clump, scraping down the bowl several times.
3. Press the dough evenly into the prepared pan.
4. In a small saucepan over very low heat, stir the raspberry jam just until smooth. Spread the jam evenly over the unbaked layer in the pan.
5. Sprinkle the reserved flour mixture evenly over the jam.
6. Bake for 23 to 27 minutes, until the topping is lightly browned. Let the pan cool completely on a wire rack. Run a sharp knife around the edge of the pan, then cut into 25 squares (5 squares by 5 squares).

Pine Nut–Orange Bars

Treat yourself and your guests to these orange-flavored bars topped with a scrumptious mixture of marmalade, pine nuts, and a dash of dark rum.

1¾ cups flour
1 teaspoon baking powder
¼ teaspoon salt
1 teaspoon grated orange rind
¾ cup (1½ sticks) unsalted butter,
   at room temperature

¾ cup sugar
1 egg
½ cup orange marmalade
1 tablespoon dark rum
¾ cup pine nuts (pignoli)

1. Preheat the oven to 375°F; grease a 9 × 9-inch baking pan. In a small bowl, stir or whisk together the flour, baking powder, salt, and grated orange rind.

2. In a large bowl, cream the butter and sugar. Add the egg and beat well. Gradually add the flour mixture, blending well after each addition.

3. Spread the batter evenly in the prepared pan.

4. Bake for 18 to 22 minutes, until the top is lightly browned and a toothpick inserted in the center of the pan comes out clean. Allow the pan to cool completely on a wire rack.

5. In a small saucepan over low heat, stir the marmalade and rum until smooth. Remove from the heat and stir in the pine nuts. Spread the marmalade mixture over the baked layer in the pan and allow to cool. Run a sharp knife around the edge of the pan, then cut into 20 bars (4 bars by 5 bars).

Gingerbread Bars with Pecan-Bourbon Topping

Plenty of pungent spices (see page 71 for information about spices), good molasses, and a lick of coffee make this gingerbread bar a favorite—and the tipsy topping gives it a moist, rich finish.

For the bottom layer:
½ cup unsulphured molasses (not blackstrap)
¼ cup boiling water
¼ cup hot coffee
½ teaspoon baking soda
2 cups flour
½ teaspoon salt
2 teaspoons cinnamon
1½ teaspoons ground ginger
½ teaspoon ground allspice
½ teaspoon ground cloves
½ cup (1 stick) unsalted butter, at room temperature
1 cup sugar
1 egg

For the topping:
¼ cup (½ stick) unsalted butter
¼ cup light corn syrup
¼ cup bourbon
½ cup confectioners' sugar, sifted
¾ cup chopped toasted pecans

1. Preheat the oven to 350°F; grease and flour a 9 × 13-inch baking pan. In a medium-size bowl, stir together the molasses, water, and coffee; add the baking soda and stir to dissolve; allow to cool. In another medium-size bowl, stir or whisk together the flour, salt, and spices.

2. In a large bowl, cream the butter and sugar. Add the egg and beat well. Add the molasses mixture and the flour mixture alternately, in three parts each, blending well after each addition.

3. Pour the batter evenly into the prepared pan.

4. Bake for 21 to 25 minutes, until the top is dry and a toothpick inserted in the center of the pan comes out clean. Let the pan cool slightly on a wire rack.

5. Make the topping: In a heavy saucepan over low heat, combine the butter, corn syrup, and bourbon, stirring until melted and well blended. Remove from the heat and beat in the confectioners' sugar. Stir in the pecans.

6. Spread the topping evenly over the baked gingerbread layer in the pan. Pierce the gingerbread with a wooden skewer, making holes a little less than an inch apart; the topping will seep into the holes. Let the topping cool completely. Run a sharp knife around the edge of the pan, then cut into 28 squares (4 squares by 7 squares)

Hot Tips: Chips

Should the day come when you tire of chocolate chips in your bar cookies, consider substituting one of these alternative "chips." The amount (as specified in the recipe) stays the same; only the flavor changes.

- Chopped pecans, almonds, pistachios, walnuts, peanuts, hazelnuts, pine nuts, or macadamias
- Dark or light raisins
- Currants
- Chopped dried apricots, cherries, cranberries, peaches, figs, pineapple, or apple
- Chocolate-covered raisins or peanuts, chopped or whole
- Toffee crunch candy bars, broken or chopped
- Peanut candy bars, chopped

Glazes

Glazes are the finishing touches for bar cookies. Spread your choice of glaze over an uncut pan of cookies either to add pizazz or as a base for decorations—see page 76 for simple decorating ideas that begin with a layer of glaze.

If you prepare glaze ahead and you're not using it immediately, cover with a piece of plastic wrap placed directly on the surface of the glaze.

Tip: Glaze may take quite a while to set at room temperature, especially in hot or humid weather. To speed up the process, cover the glazed, uncut pan of cookies with plastic wrap and refrigerate until the glaze is firm.

Vanilla Glaze

MAKES ABOUT 1 CUP

1 ½ tablespoons unsalted butter, melted
1 ½ teaspoons vanilla extract

¼ cup milk or heavy cream
2 cups sifted confectioners' sugar
2 pinches of salt

Stir together the melted butter, vanilla, and milk (or cream). Add the confectioners' sugar and salt and beat for about 4 minutes. If necessary, thin with a little more milk or cream, or thicken with a bit more confectioners' sugar.

This glaze sets and dries quickly. To prevent a crust from forming, cover the unused portion with a piece of plastic wrap pressed directly onto the surface of the glaze.

Semisweet Chocolate Glaze

MAKES ABOUT 1¼ CUPS

1½ ounces unsweetened chocolate, chopped
3 tablespoons unsalted butter
¼ cup heavy cream

1 teaspoon vanilla extract
2 cups sifted confectioners' sugar
Pinch of salt

Melt the chocolate and butter either in a medium-size bowl resting on a saucepan holding a few inches of simmering water or in a saucepan large enough to contain all the ingredients. Stir until smooth. Turn off the heat. Add the remaining ingredients and beat until smooth. If necessary, thin with a little more cream or thicken with more confectioners' sugar.

Bittersweet Chocolate Glaze

MAKES ABOUT 1 CUP

3 ounces unsweetened chocolate, chopped

6 ounces semisweet chocolate, chopped

4 teaspoons neutral vegetable oil (corn, safflower, canola, or sunflower)

Melt the chocolate with the oil in a heavy saucepan over very low heat, stirring until smooth.

Mocha Glaze

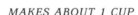

MAKES ABOUT 1 CUP

2 ounces unsweetened chocolate, chopped

2 tablespoons unsalted butter

¼ cup strong coffee

½ teaspoon vanilla extract

1 ⅓ cups sifted confectioners' sugar

Pinch of salt

In a small saucepan over low heat, stir the chocolate and butter until melted and blended. Transfer to a large bowl, add the coffee and vanilla, and stir again. Add the confectioners' sugar and salt and beat until smooth. If necessary, thin with a little more coffee or thicken with a little more confectioners' sugar.

Lemon Glaze

MAKES ABOUT 1 CUP

¼ cup fresh lemon juice
2 teaspoons water
1 teaspoon grated lemon rind

1 tablespoon unsalted butter,
    melted and cooled
3¼ cups sifted confectioners' sugar

In a large bowl, stir all the ingredients together. Beat until smooth. If necessary, add a bit more water to thin the glaze or more confectioners' sugar to thicken it.

Rum Glaze

MAKES ABOUT 1 CUP

¼ cup light rum
1 teaspoon vanilla extract
1 tablespoon unsalted butter, at
    room temperature

2½ cups sifted confectioners' sugar
Pinch of salt

In a large bowl, stir all the ingredients together. Beat until smooth. If necessary, thin with a little more rum or thicken with a little more confectioners' sugar.

Butterscotch Glaze

3 tablespoons unsalted butter
6 tablespoons packed light brown sugar
4½ tablespoons heavy cream
1½ cups sifted confectioners' sugar
Pinch of salt

Combine the butter, brown sugar, and cream in a heavy saucepan over low heat and cook, stirring constantly, until the butter and brown sugar are completely melted. Remove from the heat and allow to cool to warm. Add the confectioners' sugar and salt and beat until smooth.

Index